The Clinton Scandals
and the Politics of
Image Restoration

Recent Titles in the
Praeger Series in Political Communication
Robert E. Denton, Jr., *General Editor*

The Clinton Scandals and the Politics of Image Restoration

Joseph R. Blaney and William L. Benoit

Praeger Series in Political Communication

PRAEGER

Westport, Connecticut
London

Library of Congress Cataloging-in-Publication Data

Blaney, Joseph R.
 The Clinton scandals and the politics of image restoration / Joseph R. Blaney and William L. Benoit.
  p. cm.—(Praeger series in political communication, ISSN 1062–5623)
  Includes bibliographical references and index.
  ISBN 0–275–97106–6 (alk. paper)
  1. Clinton, Bill, 1946—Oratory. 2. Clinton, Bill, 1946—Language. 3. Clinton, Bill, 1946—Public opinion. 4. Scandals—United States—History—20th century. 5. Political corruption—United States—History—20th century. 6. United States—Politics and government—1993– 7. Rhetoric—Political aspects—United States—History—20th century. 8. Communication in politics—United States—History—20th century. 9. Public opinion—United States—History—20th century. 10. Political oratory—United States—History—20th century. I. Benoit, William L. II. Title. III. Series.
  E886.2.B59 2001
  973.929′092—dc21   00–044130

British Library Cataloguing in Publication Data is available.

Library of Congress Catalog Card Number: 00–044130
ISBN: 0–275–97106–6
ISSN: 1062–5623

First published in 2001

Praeger Publishers, 88 Post Road West, Westport, CT 06881
An imprint of Greenwood Publishing Group, Inc.
www.praeger.com

Printed in the United States of America

The paper used in this book complies with the Permanent Paper Standard issued by the National Information Standards Organization (Z39.48–1984).

10 9 8 7 6 5 4 3 2 1

Contents

Series Foreword

Those of us from the discipline of communication studies have long believed that communication is prior to all other fields of inquiry. In several other forums I have argued that the essence of politics is "talk" or human interaction.[1] Such interaction may be formal or informal, verbal or nonverbal, public or private, but it is always persuasive, forcing us consciously or subconsciously to interpret, to evaluate, and to act. Communication is the vehicle for human action.

From this perspective, it is not surprising that Aristotle recognized the natural kinship of politics and communication in his writings *Politics* and *Rhetoric*. In the former, he established that humans are "political beings, [who] alone of the animals [are] furnished with the faculty of language."[2] In the latter, he began his systematic analysis of discourse by proclaiming that "rehetorical study, in its strict sense, is concerned with the modes of persuasion."[3] Thus, it was recognized over twenty-three hundred years ago that politics and communication go hand in hand because they are essential parts of human nature.

In 1981, Dan Nimmo and Keith Sanders proclaimed that political communication was an emerging field.[4] Although its origin, as noted, dates back centuries, a "self-consciously cross-disciplinary" focus began in the late 1950s. Thousands of books and articles later, colleges and universities offer a variety of graduate and undergraduate coursework in the area in such diverse departments as communication, mass communication, journalism, political science, and sociology.[5] In Nimmo and Sander's early assessment, the "key areas of inquiry" included rhetori-

cal analysis, propaganda analysis, attitude change studies, voting studies, government and the news media, functional and systems analyses,
technological changes, media technologies, campaign techniques, and
research techniques.[6] In a survey of the state of the field in 1983, the
same authors and Lynda Kaid found additional, more specific areas of
concerns such as the presidency, political polls, public opinion, debates,
and advertising.[7] Since the first study, they have also noted a shift away
from the rather behavioral approach.

A decade later, Dan Nimmo and David Swanson argued that "political
communication has developed some identity as a more or less distinct domain of scholarly work."[8] The scope and concerns of the area have further
expanded to include critical theories and cultural studies. Although there is
no precise definition, method, or disciplinary home of the area of inquiry,
its primary domain comprises the role, processes, and effects of communication within the context of politics broadly defined.

In 1985, the editors of *Political Communication Yearbook: 1984* noted
that "more things are happening in the study, teaching, and practice of political communication than can be captured within the space limitations of the
relatively few publication available."[9] In addition, they argued that the
backgrounds of "those involved in the field [are] so varied and pluralist in
outlook and approach, . . . it [is] a mistake to adhere slavishly to any set for-
mat in shaping the content."[10] More recently, Swanson and Nimmo have
called for "ways of overcoming the unhappy consequences of fragmenta-
tion within a framwork that respects, encourages, and benefits from diverse
scholarly commitments, agendas, and approaches."[11]

In agreement with these assessments of the area and with gentle encouragement, in 1988 Praeger established the series entitled "Praeger Series in
Political Communication." The series is open to all qualitative and
quantitive methodologies as well as contemporary and historical studies.
The key to characterizing the studies in the series is the focus on communication variables or activities within a political context or dimension. As of
this writing, over seventy volumes have been published and numerous impressive works are forthcoming. Scholars from the disciplines of communication, history, journalism, political science, and sociology have
participated in the series.

I am, without shame or modesty, a fan of the series. The joy of serving as
its editor is in participating in the dialogue of the field of political communication and in reading the contributors' works. I invite you to join me.

Robert E. Denton, Jr.

NOTES

1. See Robert E. Denton, Jr., *The Symbolic Dimensions of the American Presidency* (Prospect Heights, IL: Waveland Press, 1982); Robert E. Denton, Jr., and Gary Woodward, *Political Communication in America* (New York: Praeger, 1985; 2d ed., 1990); Robert E. Denton, Jr., and Dan Hahn, *Presidential Communication* (New York: Praeger, 1986); and Robert E. Denton Jr., *The Primetime Presidency of Ronald Regan* (New York: Praeger, 1988).

2. Aristotle, *The Politics of Aristotle*, trans. Ernest Barker (New York: Oxford University Press, 1970), p. 5.

3. Aristotle, *Rhetoric*, trans. W. Rhys Roberts (New York: The Modern Library, 1954), p. 22.

4. Dan Nimmo and Keith Sanders, "Introduction: The Emergence of Political Communication as a Field," in *Handbook of Political Communication*, eds Dan Nimmo and Keith Sanders (Beverly Hills, CA: Sage, 1981), pp. 11–36.

5. Ibid., p. 15.

6. Ibid., pp. 17–27.

7. Keith Sanders, Lynda Kaid, and Dan Nimmo, eds. *Political Communication Yearbook: 1984* (Carbondale, IL: Southern Illinois University: 1985), pp. 283–308.

8. Dan Nimmo and David Swanson, "The Field of Political Communication: Beyond the Voter Persuasion Paradigm," in *New Directions in Political Communication*, eds. David Swanson and Dan Nimmo (Beverly Hills, CA: Sage, 1990), p. 8.

9. Sanders, Kaid, and Nimmo, *Political Communication Yearbook: 1984*, p. xiv.

10. Ibid.

11. Nimmo and Swanson, "The Field of Political Communication," p. 11.

Preface

The subject of this book, President Bill Clinton, has been more than generous in providing fodder for an examination of image restoration in politics. His accusers have also done their part in making the public aware of Mr. Clinton's real and perceived shortcomings. Indeed, as will be discussed later, Bill Clinton has been the subject of a tremendous amount of scrutiny by his personal and political enemies.

ACKNOWLEDGMENTS

I am very grateful to many people for their professional and personal support throughout this exhausting project. Beginning at the professional level, I owe more thanks than could be expressed in this space to my advisor and coauthor William L. Benoit. His scholarly encouragement has been exemplary. It is no exaggeration to say that he would return drafts of my dissertation chapters (with suggested revisions) within hours of my submitting them. His enthusiasm for this project was the driving force behind its timely completion. His contribution to the original dissertation was so profound that he rightly is my coauthor for this book.

I am also thankful that Bill has included me in his program of political communication research, which has led to several books, articles and presentations. Because of his mentoring, I am entering the communication discipline with a solid foundation. He is a friend and family-oriented man whom I admire very much.

I would also like to thank others at the University of Missouri: Pamela Benoit, Richard Hardy, Michael Kramer, and Michael Porter. They were kind enough to accommodate scheduling needs under short notice. Moreover, their feedback proved invaluable to this work.

The Department of Communication at the University of Missouri provided me with financial support and the opportunity to teach for three years. The department secretaries, Maureen "Mo" Kremer and Jodie Lenser, were always looking out for me, making sure that I had my bureaucratic materials in order. They made my stay at "Mizzou" a pleasant experience.

Of course, my classmates in the program at Missouri provided needed encouragement at one moment, and riotous laughter at another. Intellectually, I was the least among them. They lifted me up. I dare not begin to list names for fear of excluding someone. Virtually all of them helped me in some fashion.

The Department of Mass Communication at Northwest Missouri State University has been most helpful as well. Jerry Donnelly, my chair, and Ron DeYoung, my dean, were generous with their financial and professional support. Marla McCrary was a very helpful department secretary. Likewise, I am thankful for my new colleagues at Illinois State University. Graduate students Sara Joyce and Jennifer Moore offered research assistance.

At the personal level, my greatest thanks goes to my wife, Lauri Blaney. She managed to support our family financially and in every other way during my doctoral studies. On most evenings, she had to go to sleep without her husband, who was up studying and writing until hours later. I admire her strength and she has my eternal love and devotion.

Thanks goes also to my "Love Bug," Maggie Blaney. On those evenings when she would wake in the middle of the night and come kiss and hug her laboring Daddy, I felt like the stress of the program was nonexistent. Her love is a miracle. Also, my toddler son Matthew Blaney has provided much joy and happiness.

My siblings and their spouses were supportive throughout this writing as well, covering family responsibilities on my behalf. They include: Mary and Del Rychener, Margaret and Jonathan Farley, Bridget Blaney, and Rick, Janet, and Olivia Blaney. In addition to my immediate family, the extended Maglio family has treated me like one of their own.

My family's beloved parish, Sacred Heart Catholic Church, was nurturing and engaging throughout our time in Columbia. Likewise, my pals at Knights of Columbus Council 1529 provided an outlet for meaningful activity when off campus.

Ellen Blaney, also known as Mom, gave me encouragement, love, and confidence from my childhood until her death in June 1998. She was a truly Christian woman. My thanks go to her and my deceased father, Dr. Richard Blaney, for their gifts of life, faith, and hope.

To the Lord Jesus I offer thanks for his grace, sustenance, and his Holy Cross. AMDG.

Joseph R. Blaney

I would like to thank my wife, Pam, and my daughter, Jen, for their un-failing love and support. They are also both willing to discuss my research and offer me their considerable insights. I also want to thank Joe Blaney. He worked hard, had original ideas, asked interesting and challenging ques-tions, and listened to my advice—but didn't slavishly follow me. He made advising a true pleasure. I also want to thank my teachers at Wayne State University, who started me on the path I now tread.

William L. Benoit

Chapter One

Introduction: Why Study Clinton's Image Repair?

The *apologia* of the president of the United States facing serious allegations merits scholarly attention. When charges of wrongdoing befuddle the chief executive, much is at stake (Gergen, 1998).

A president who has come under attack for scandalous behavior is likely to be distracted from the duties of commander-in-chief of the U.S. Armed Forces. In a dangerous world filled with nuclear, biological, and chemical weapons, reasoned and deliberate responses to crises are imperative. As such, situations that compel a president to take politically expedient, yet ill-advised, measures need to be avoided. In short, the president needs to maintain a positive image in order to act freely and responsibly on the world stage.

An embattled and weakened president could not function effectively on the domestic front if he were distracted either. With a reputation damaged by a scandal, a president may lack the political clout to pass needed legislation or to sustain the veto of harmful legislative acts. Moreover, the president's ability to act effectively on unpopular yet necessary measures would be diminished.

So, the question arises, "Do we want our Chief Executive and Commander-in-Chief distracted by scandal when facing decisions of great domestic and foreign importance?" Regardless of one's ideological leanings the answer ought to be "no," because potential problems affecting all Americans might develop without recourse to the best possible decisions. There is no implicit assumption in that question that places the president above the laws of the country. Nor does the question mean that a president should not be investigated. The concern merely recognizes that a distracted president could be detrimental to the nation.

Of course, the aforementioned factors are only policy-related reasons for attending to the president's image. Television shows devoted to Bill Clinton's alleged social, sexual, and financial misdeeds have been rewarded with ratings windfalls (Baker & Bard, 1998). As Rose (1997) noted:

> President Clinton is besieged with accusations of financial impropriety and sexual harassment during his tenure as governor of Arkansas. Questions from the press routinely inundate Clinton regarding these personal matters. Such probing into pre-presidential conduct is without precedent in the history of American politics. (p. 32)

The public's extreme interest in scandal in general (and sexual indiscretions in particular) compels inquiry as well. Therefore, scholars have an interest in examining the discourse of presidents and other powerful officials when their character or actions come under attack from the public, media, and partisan opponents.

This book will examine President Bill Clinton's image repair discourse in the wake of various moral and legal accusations against him. Specifically, we will examine rhetoric related to charges that Clinton (1) abused illegal drugs (marijuana), (2) acted illegally as governor of Arkansas in a real estate transaction now commonly known as "Whitewater," (3) committed adultery (before his 1992 election), (4) evaded military conscription, and (5) had an illicit sexual relationship with White House intern Monica Lewinsky, simultaneously suborning perjury and obstructing justice regarding the alleged affair. In addition to Clinton's discourse, we will examine the persuasive defense strategies of his surrogates prompted by these allegations as well as accusations following unwarranted requests for FBI files ("Filegate") and the White House Travel Office firings ("Travelgate"). Clinton has not offered substantial discourse concerning these matters.

This study begins with a review of the scholarly literature on the topic: political *apologia* and Bill Clinton. From there, the purpose of the study will be explained and specific research questions offered. Next, Benoit's (1995a) theory of image restoration strategies will be explicated, including a review of literature employing that method. After this, the method will be applied to the aforementioned allegations, with evaluations of effectiveness offered in each study. Finally, an assessment of the study's theoretical contribution will be offered.

POLITICAL *APOLOGIA*

There is a respectable body of research devoted to political *apologia*. Linkugel and Razak (1969) examined former U.S. Representative and Tennessee Governor Sam Houston's persuasive defense following charges that he breached a member's privileges by severely beating Congressman William Stanberry in 1832. Houston argued that he had been provoked by his victim, Ohio Representative William Stanberry. Stanberry had written an article in the *National Intelligencer* accusing Houston of governmental corruption. Stanberry would not even answer inquiries as to why such charges were leveled. Moreover, Houston made an important distinction: he had assaulted Stanberry for words *published,* not words spoken as a privileged member on the floor of the U.S. House of Representatives. As such, the government had no legal case against him. Moreover, Houston placed the struggle in the context of "unyielding privilege [represented by Stanberry] and the basic rights of the common man [namely, Houston]" (p. 269). Linkugel and Razak found that Houston not only effectively defended himself from the immediate charge, but used the spectacle of the charges as a platform to rehabilitate his declining image among citizens of the country. He eventually became a United States senator.

Senator Edward Kennedy has been the subject of study as well. Ling (1970) examined Kennedy's televised address following his automobile accident on Chappaquiddick Island that killed Mary Jo Kopechne. Employing a Burkean analysis, Ling found that Kennedy portrayed himself as the victim not only of the pentadic scene, but possibly of the negative reaction to the accident. He concluded that the speech succeeded in securing Kennedy's job as senator from Massachussetts. Benoit (1988) also examined Kennedy's Chappaquiddick speech about the fatal crash and subsequent failure in reporting the accident. Kennedy shifted the blame for the crash to the road conditions (similar to the notion of "scene" in the pentadic analysis). He shifted the blame again by attributing the failure to report the incident to the concussion and exhaustion suffered in the crash and attempts to save Kopechne. Benoit found that these strategies were sufficient to keep his U.S. Senate seat, but not effective enough to remove all blemishes, and thus precluded a successful presidential bid.

The Watergate scandal (as will be shown in the next section) has provided much material for analysis. Kahl (1984) examined the *apologia* of Watergate figure John Dean in his books *Blind Ambition* and *Lost Honor.* Dean used the strategies of denial, differentiation, and transcendence in order to achieve a form of rhetorical absolution. Kahl discovered that written *apologia* (such as in a book) provides distinctive elements for critics to consider about persuasive discourse. She recommended that we distinguish between written and spoken *apologia* in order to advance a "more sophisticated and comprehensive" approach to such analysis (p. 250). Gold (1978) argued that the Watergate scandal impacted persuasive defense discourse in the 1976 presidential election. The defense of one's character became more important because honesty became such an important issue and because the media became more aggressive in their pursuit of corruption after the Nixon debacle. Also, the presence of an aggressive and skeptical media meant an end to the days of a single speech or set of speeches serving as a complete *apologia* campaign. The media's demand for interaction and its constant evaluation and scrutiny required a constant flow of defensive discourse.

The actions of U.S. Representatives have been scrutinized as well. Morello (1979) studied the apology of Ohio Congressman Wayne Hays for keeping a mistress (Elizabeth Ray), lying about the affair, and paying for the mistress's salary with public revenues. He found that Hays' speech went further in saving his marriage than preserving his political career, which constituted a rhetorical choice. For example, Hays paid more attention to private affairs when he admitted the affair but claimed it occurred when he was "legally separated and single" (p. 23). Also, Morello found that Hays employed the "juxtaposition technique" when he chose to avoid his usual inflammatory style of official address in favor of a more subdued explanation of what had occurred in what should have been (Hays implied) his private life. Hays also indicated the importance of his marriage over his career when he said, "Six weeks ago I was married to the woman I love more than anything in this world, including this house" (p. 23). Although Hays did ultimately resign his seat, his replacement (Rep. Carl Albert) verified that Hays' genuine rhetorical goal was saving his marriage.

Short (1987) studied the *apologia* of Idaho Congressman George Hansen following his conviction on four counts of false disclosures on his required federal documents. Hansen's use of the "paranoid" style (where the supposed motives of attackers provide ironic support for the target) was effective in his 1984 reelection campaign. Though he lost the contest, the tiny 150-vote margin of loss indicates an effective defense for a multiple-convictions felon. Collins and Clark (1992) studied former U.S. Speaker of the House Jim Wright's resignation speech following charges of political corruption. They found that he sought to increase the public's perception of Congress as corrupt itself, which would make his improprieties less offensive. This only served to de-legitimize the institution of Congress further and left Wright's image still damaged.

Finally, Kennedy and Benoit (1997) analyzed U.S. House of Representatives Speaker Newt Gingrich's image repair strategies following attacks on his acceptance of a lucrative book contract. He employed strategies of denial, good intentions, bolstering, attacking accuser, and corrective action. Kennedy and Benoit found his discourse ineffective as evidenced by the attacks that lingered after the scandal was presumably behind him. They also noted a low public approval rating as an indicator of poor persuasive defense. This study further illustrated how political figures may choose to defend themselves rhetorically.

The review of political *apologia* shows that political rhetors can successfully defend themselves by differentiating what they did from what they were accused of doing (such as in the cases of Sam Houston and Wayne Hays). Also, the studies of Ted Kennedy's discourse following the Chappaquiddick incident show that blaming the situation one had to deal with can be effective as well. Attacking one's accuser can be effective in some instances (such as Rep. George Hansen's almost-successful reelection bid) but ineffective in others (such as House Speakers Wright and Gingrich's predicaments).

PRESIDENTIAL *APOLOGIA*

Presidential *apologia* studies have concerned themselves with three individuals: Richard Nixon, Ronald Reagan, and Bill Clinton. The studies are reviewed in that order.

The bulk of presidential *apologia* has examined Richard Nixon. Brummett (1975) found that Nixon was in a "rhetorical bind from which he could not escape" (p. 257) during the Watergate scandal. The scandal involved accusations that he orchestrated, and later attempted to cover up, a break-in at the Democratic National Headquarters. Nixon's strategy of asking the public to consider the virtues of his presidency rather than the demonstrated vices of his person was ineffective because it defined him in less human terms, a humanity which he needed for persuasive identification.

Harrell, Ware, and Linkugel (1975) divided Nixon's Watergate discourse into two phases: explanation and absolution. In the explanation phase he sought to explicate how he could justify initial statements about the absolute innocence of his staff with the eventual resignation of four of those staff personnel. In the absolution stage he denied any involvement in the Watergate break-in and any subsequent attempt to cover it up. He also chose to differentiate between any staffers who had been involved with the break-in from those who had national security assignments.

There were three "specific weaknesses" in Nixon's *apologia* of May 22, 1974 (p. 255). First, his personal statement of "absolution" came too late. Second, his attempts to absolve his aides weakened his position when it became clear that they were, indeed, involved. Finally, his use of a press release for his crucial, early responses had a smaller audience than a television press conference would have had.

With his popularity at record low levels, Nixon's address to the nation on August 15, 1974, was crucial. He continued denying involvement with any illegal activities before or after the infamous break-in. He also differentiated between his taking responsibility for the incident and admitting any personal role. Finally, Nixon used transcendence when he "asked the nation to put Watergate behind them. Vitally needed domestic legislation was going unattended" (p. 258). In short, the scandal should not have been so important because the country faced larger problems. Harrell, Ware, and Linkugel concluded that Nixon's Watergate *apologia* failed. They said that he failed to create "an image of the strong and independent leader acting upon the scene" (p. 260). As such, he did not appear to be in control of the rhetorical situation.

Benoit (1982) found that Nixon used nine persuasive defense strategies in the wake of the Watergate scandal. First, he made public pronouncements to the effect that he was ensuring a full and complete investigation of the incident. Second, he shifted the blame for the break-in and cover-up to his staff. Third, Nixon attempted to get the public to shift its attention away from Watergate, saying that the matter consumed too much of his attention which was needed for other more pressing matters. Benoit called this strategy *minimization*. Fourth, Nixon criticized the credibility of John Dean, who was the only member of his administration to disagree with Nixon's denials of knowledge of a cover-up. Fifth, he "attempted to justify his refusal to turn over materials" by placing importance on the concept of confidentiality between himself and his advisors (p. 197). Sixth, he pointed to the electoral "mandate" from the previous year as evidence that the public supported him. Seventh, Nixon claimed to be cooperating fully with the special prosecutors, turning over documents and recordings as requested. He underscored his cooperative attitude by alluding to his voluntary actions in this regard. Eighth, Nixon claimed "executive privilege," the concept that the details of official conversations between the president and his staff cannot be legally subpoenaed. This differed from his earlier claim of confidentiality, which was a less legalistic characterization of his preferred treatment of the conversations. Finally, he made use of the infamous secret tapes of his conversations with staff members. He used them first to discredit John Dean's damaging testimony and then again to bolster his descriptions of the Watergate scandal's subsequent proceedings among the president and his cabinet. Benoit found that Nixon's discourse failed to reverse a negative public opinion that accompanied revelations of the misfeasance.

Vartabedian (1985) examined Nixon's *apologia* in both the "Checkers" speech and Watergate scandal. He concluded that Nixon had to confront directly the financial accusations in 1952 in order to stay on Eisenhower's ticket, and that he did so appropriately. Also, Nixon's ineffective use of bolstering and differentiation in the Watergate affair were in contrast with effective denials in the "Checkers" speech.

Nixon also engaged in persuasive defense over his Vietnam policies. Newman (1970) examined Nixon's speech of November 3, 1969, regarding his "secret" plan for peace in Vietnam. He found that the speech did not meet its expectations, as the event was announced weeks earlier and received much hype. Newman claimed that "neither his rhetorical strategies nor his substantive argument[s]" were strong and appropriate to the occasion (p. 178). Notably, Newman asserts that Nixon maintained a civil rhetorical style during this period, with Vice President Spiro Agnew acting as a more verbally aggressive surrogate.

Benoit (1995a) analyzed President Nixon's persuasive defense following attacks that he had violated his stated intention of not expanding American involvement in the Vietnam War. His order of military operations in Cambodia prompted the criticism.

In this crisis, Nixon employed bolstering by comparing himself to statesmen of America's past. He differentiated the new initiative from invasion of another country (Cambodia) by describing the initiative as a continuation of the previous policy of attacking the North Vietnamese enemy where they were. Finally, he transcended when he said the new actions were about the larger issue of ending the war rather than expanding it. Benoit pointed to polling data that showed a lack of support for the actions even after Nixon's defensive address as support that the discourse was not particularly effective.

Katula (1975) rated Nixon's eventual resignation speech as poor. Further, he points to the address as another example of "decay in the art of apologizing" (p. 5). Moreover, the speech did not allow the country to put the scandal behind it because the events which caused the resignation were not adequately addressed. Wilson (1976) found that Nixon's Watergate *apologia* could only have been effective with his die-hard loyalists because he failed to publicly recognize the seriousness of his misfeasance.

Examining an earlier Nixon, McGuckin (1968) studied Nixon's infamous "Checkers" speech from the 1952 election, which was a response to allegations that he was using a "slush fund" to live beyond the means of his Senate salary. Using a values analysis, McGuckin concluded that Nixon's speech was effective in convincing voters that he was morally solid because Nixon identified himself with the audience's favored values.

Rosenfield (1968) examined the discourse of Nixon and former President Harry S Truman simultaneously and saw four analogous qualities, which could be descriptive of other rhetors' discourse. First, *apologia* that is broadcast is "likely to be a part of a short, intense, decisive clash of views" (p. 449). Second, when using broadcast media to engage in persuasive defense, the rhetor will probably choose to attack as well. Third, the discussion of facts relevant to the *apologia* is placed in the middle third of the speeches. Fourth, the rhetor under attack will use elements of earlier discourse when composing *apologia* intended for a nationwide audience.

Another president who came under attack for misconduct was Ronald Reagan. Benoit, Gullifor, and Panici (1991) studied President Ronald Reagan's defensive discourse in the wake of the Iran-Contra scandal. Reagan had been accused of violating his policy of not negotiating with terrorists after it was discovered that the United States sold arms to Iran in exchange for the release of hostages. His defense strategies were framed in a discussion of hostages. The first phase concentrated on denial of a deal of arms for hostages. The second phase consisted of Reagan claiming that his actions resulted from good intentions. Finally, he admitted to making the deal and proposed corrective action. The authors found that Reagan's discourse eventually led to a rebound in the job approval ratings he lost after the scandal was discovered. However, the ratings never were as high as they had been prior to the scandal. Furthermore, they argue that Reagan would have been more successful if he had admitted wrongdoing at the start and promised corrective action.

Abadi (1990) examined the political *apologia* of President Ronald Reagan following the Tower Commission's report on his involvement in the Iran-Contra scandal. The author proposed a model of *apologia* that begins with an acknowledgment of responsibility (full or partial) and moves on to various sub-strategies appropriate to the amount of responsibility admitted. No subsequent applications of this method have been found.

More recently, President Bill Clinton's defensive discourse has been analyzed. Benoit and Wells (1998) examined the *apologia* of Bill Clinton and First Lady Hillary Rodham Clinton regarding the Whitewater land deal in Arkansas. In a 1994 press conference, President Clinton's strategies centered on bolstering, praising his foreign and domestic accomplishments as well as claiming to cooperate with the special prosecutor. Clinton also denied a number of allegations, including owing back taxes, using federally insured loan money in his gubernatorial campaigns, and earning a profit from the failed Whitewater land deal. He shifted the blame when he claimed that others were responsible for the record-keeping of the financial dealings. Finally, he used transcendence to place the Whitewater issue in a larger context: The deal took place sixteen years earlier and surely was not relevant to the issues facing his presidency. He also denied wrongdoing by Hillary during the press conference.

In a *New York Times* advertisement entitled "We Interrupt this Newspaper to Give You the Facts," Clinton defenders collectively denied (1) having used a savings and loan to finance their investment, (2) defaulting on the loan, (3) going into business with an S & L director, (4) trying to influence savings and loan regulators, and (5) representing Madison S & L through Hillary's law firm. The ad attempted to bolster Hillary's image by pointing to her work to reform health care. The defenders attacked their accusers by describing the accusations as personal and claimed she was being attacked because of her health care role. Finally, transcendence was employed when the ad asserted that it was time to deal with other issues facing the country.

Mrs. Clinton contributed to her defense with her own press conference. She engaged in denial when she said she had not received special treatment in receiving commodities futures investment advice. She shifted the blame for her unusual financial transactions when she said she opened the account at the recommendation of her friend Jim Blair. She attempted to bolster herself when she spoke of their "having nothing to hide" (p. 11). On multiple occasions during the press conference she referred to her openness regarding the issue. Transcendence was used again when she implored the public to give more attention to "more important" matters. Regarding the Clintons' tendency to change the details of their explanation, she employed defeasibility, saying that the episode had occurred so long ago that the recollection of events was difficult. Finally, she attacked her accusers as people more concerned with destroying the Clintons than building up the country.

Benoit and Wells found that the press conferences and the *New York Times* advertisement used to deflect criticism were effective, with the president's discourse being more effective than the First Lady's utterances. Public opinion polls supported this assessment.

Carlin and Howard (1994) found that Clinton successfully rebounded to a second, nonconsecutive term as governor of Arkansas in 1984 (recall that Clinton had lost his gubernatorial reelection bid in 1980) due in part to his effective *apologia*. They concluded that his apology (in the form of mortification) for mistakes made in his first term allowed him to move on to communicate his plans as a candidate. They also held that Clinton's political battles in Arkansas fine-tuned his rhetorical abilities for the 1992 presidential election. For instance, Clinton learned to "translate issues of national importance into clear and highly personal anecdotes" (p. 21). Moreover, many of the issues he had talked about previously in Arkansas appeared on his presidential campaign agenda.

Marlow (1994) studied Clinton's discourse in the wake of allegations that he committed adultery and evaded the draft. She found that differentiation as understood by Ware and Linkugel (1973) "seems to be an especially prominent strategy in Clinton's apologies" (p. 157). For instance, in 1969, Clinton wrote a letter which appeared to be an example of someone slyly manipulating his draft status in order to avoid military service. However, he differentiated the letter from a draft-dodging document by calling it a sincere communication from a young man of deep conviction. Likewise, when accused of adultery, Clinton differentiated himself as a "husband who has made mistakes" rather than an unfaithful husband (p. 158).

The studies of presidential *apologia* demonstrate that various strategies can be effective in persuasive defense. Richard Nixon's use of denial of wrongdoing in his "Checkers" speech was effective but ineffective in the Watergate matter. Bolstering one's public performance can be effective (such as in Clinton's Whitewater discourse) or ineffective (such as in Nixon's Watergate and Vietnam controversies). Reagan demonstrated the effectiveness of admitting wrongdoing in the name of good intentions combined with a promise of corrective action. Finally, one should note that Clinton has proved to be adept at *apologia* by using mortification, bolstering, denial, blame shifting, and attacks on accusers to defend himself from accusations of wrongdoing.

OTHER RHETORICAL STUDIES OF BILL CLINTON

Aside from *apologia* studies, there has been much written about Clinton's rhetorical nature. For instance, Brenders and Fabj (1993) found that Clinton's rhetoric in the 1992 presidential election addressed the three themes of hope, change, and unity. Also addressing themes, Getz (1994) examined Clinton's Arkansas gubernatorial inaugural addresses. In the course of five such speeches, Clinton revealed his vision for the state: a forward-looking hope, change for the better, and a government that accepts social responsibility.

Llewellyn (1994) found that Clinton effectively identified (in the Burkean sense) with voters during stump speeches in the 1992 campaign. This identification was achieved through anecdotes from his own life circumstances. Moreover, voters were invited to identify not only with Clinton himself, but also with the goals of the campaign (which, if achieved, contrasted with the country's difficulties in 1992). Meanwhile,

C. A. Smith (1994) discovered that Clinton relied on the jeremiad form of rhetoric (where there is an assumed covenant between God and his chosen people at the root of social problems) consistently, employing it for the duration of the 1992 campaign. Again, Smith (1996) repeated that Clinton's electoral success in 1992 could be attributed to "a consistent logic that exhibited all the features of the modern political jeremiad" (p. 226).

Whereas C. A. Smith saw jeremiad at play, L. D. Smith (1994) recognized a narrative structure. He found that the "telepolitical age," 1984 through the present, required candidates to present their messages as narratives for a viewing audience.

Turning attention to the subject of direct rhetorical confrontation, Herbeck (1994) noted that the importance of the 1992 presidential debates have been underrated. He pointed out that Clinton entered the debates in front of candidates Bush and Perot and won the election by a comfortable margin. However, Clinton also gave solid performances in all three debates which could have helped his cause. With the economy doing so poorly at the time, the debates stood as an opportunity for Bush to present an economic agenda appealing to the voters.

Addressing a bigger campaign picture, Seib (1994) examined Clinton's overall election cycle as a metaphorical "roller coaster" ride. Beginning with a press corps that called George Bush unbeatable in 1991, the odds were stacked against Clinton. Seib said he emerged a Democratic front-runner by default from a weak field of partisan competitors. After this, Clinton endured a series of scandals followed by recovery.

With Clinton's victory behind him, Procter and Ritter (1996) studied Clinton's presidential inauguration in 1993. They found that he engaged in a "regenerative rhetoric" that was seeking to "respond to the nation's need for a reinterpretation of its mission" (p. 13).

Denton and Holloway (1996) found that Clinton's "town hall meetings" resembled a conversation, but could not be characterized as such. The town hall forum might appear to be conversational because some of the conventional formality has been eliminated. However, the occasions are just as managed, scripted, and staged as formal addresses. Despite these limitations on true conversation, Denton and Holloway noted that the "town hall meetings" are still important because the public desires the perceived interaction and because it is "a distant approximation of true democracy, an exchange of ideas among a leader and the citizenry" (p. 36). They pointed to Clinton's *Nightline* town hall meeting with Ted Koppel as an example of the exuberance about democracy that these forums allow.

Hacker (1996) also addressed the nature of these "town hall meetings" and discovered that Clinton's use of the town hall meeting was quite intentional, not merely an attempt at populist imaging. Clinton was fully aware that his communicative strengths lie in dealing with voters directly, as opposed to dealing with the news media who were more interested in reporting on political conflict than on substantial issues.

Bostdorff (1996) found that the newly elected President Clinton dealt with the "gays in the military" issue by characteristically defining the issue in transcendent terms. He redefined the issue from a question of sexual "status" to a question of individual rights and personal conduct. As such, Bostdorff asserted that the ultimate compromise of "don't ask, don't tell" was amenable to this strategy. However, Bostdorff believed the compromise was ultimately "less than successful" because it strained relationships with the Joint Chiefs of Staff who opposed the measure and gay rights advocates who felt the policy was not much of an improvement on the status quo. Recall that Clinton had promised an end to the ban on homosexuals in the military during his campaign.

Murphy (1997) examined President Clinton's speech (in Memphis, the site of Reverend Martin Luther King's assassination) before assembled ministers of the Church of God in Christ. He found that Clinton recalled the memory of King's articulated goals and offered an assessment of how King would judge the racial situation in America. Recounting America's racial failures in the shadow of its otherwise impressive feats, Clinton embraced the themes of "family, community, work, hope, and the grace and spirit of God" as a foundation for solutions to the problems (p. 84).

Finally, Lentz (1994) studied the unusual topic of Clinton's vocal qualities. This became an issue in 1992 due to his frequent hoarseness.

The rhetorical studies of Bill Clinton demonstrate that he has been a successful orator. Although the 1992 campaign was characterized by a weak field of primary opponents and an ailing economy dogging his general election opponent, President George Bush, Clinton consistently used appropriate rhetorical strategies. His rhetorical jeremiad, which insisted on action to improve Americans' situations, was particularly appropriate during the economic recession accompanying the campaign. His rhetorical themes of hope, change, and unity were particularly attractive to voters in his campaign. Where Clinton represented hope, he was attractive to voters who felt despair. Where he represented change, Clinton became the obvious solution to problems of the present. Finally, where Clinton called for unity, he advocated attention to collective concerns, not just individual successes or failures.

SUMMARY

The review of political and presidential *apologia* and rhetorical studies of Bill Clinton reveals two major points. First, for politicians engaging in persuasive defense, denial, differentiation, shifting blame, attacking accuser, good intentions, bolstering, corrective action (promising to fix the problem), and mortification (the expression of remorse) can be effective strategies. Second, Bill Clinton has demonstrated successful rhetorical dexterity, though study of his *apologia* has been limited.

While the study of Clinton's rhetoric is fairly extensive, there remains room for much more examination. Benoit and Wells (1998) examined Clinton's image repair subsequent to accusations of financial irregularities in the Whitewater matter. However, that study was limited to press conferences (one each for Bill and Hillary) and a *New York Times* advertisement (which was not placed by Clinton). Remarks from various official functions before the press conferences could be studied as well. Seib (1994) examined Clinton's 1992 campaign as a "roller coaster" through the infidelity and draft-dodging scandals. He did an excellent job of recounting that Clinton persevered through these accusations by refocusing attention on the ailing economy. However, his study did not address image repair per se. Marlow (1994) found that Clinton employed differentiation during his 1992 campaign to answer allegations of adultery and draft-dodging. However, this study employed Ware and Linkugel's (1973) method of *apologia*. Benoit's typology of image repair is more comprehensive and could render a more complete analysis of these incidents. Finally, some controversies (e.g., Lewinsky, marijuana) have not been analyzed to date. As such, Clinton's image repair remains a fruitful area of inquiry.

GOALS OF THIS BOOK

This study will describe, analyze, and critically evaluate President Clinton's image repair strategies in six separate applications. The first purpose of this study is to discover which image restoration strategies have emerged as Bill Clinton's preferred defense utterances in the alleged matters of drug abuse, Whitewater, Gennifer Flowers, the draft, and the Monica Lewinsky/suborning perjury accusation. Second, the study seeks to evaluate the effectiveness of Clinton's discourse. Third, it desires to assess the effectiveness of the strategies employed in their given contexts. Fourth, the study would place Clinton's image repair efforts in side-by-side comparisons with other notable political orators (i.e., Reagan, Nixon, Ted Kennedy, Jim Wright). Finally, the study will probe whether there are strategic differences and similarities between Clinton and his surrogate defenders. It will examine the strategies and effectiveness of the image repair of President Bill Clinton.

The reason for choosing these particular scandals is that these have received the most attention and scrutiny in the media. One could propose to study the "haircut on the runway" matter, but the attacks for the incident subsided so quickly, probably due to the relatively trivial nature of the offense, as to lack merit for study. Also, it could be argued that Clinton's discourse in the "Filegate" and "Travelgate" matters are deserving of study. However, an extensive search shows that Clinton's surrogates have handled the vast majority, if not all, of the image repair in these matters. As such, a chapter will be devoted to studying the defense provided by surrogates in the Filegate, Travel Office, and other scandals under study here.

This study asks seven research questions:

1. Why were Clinton's image repair efforts effective or ineffective?
    a. What were the allegations he faced in each episode?
    b. Which image repair strategies were used in each episode?
    c. Was the defense effective or ineffective, and why?
2. What are the recurrent features and differences in Clinton's defenses?
3. What are the similarities and differences between defenses by Clinton and by his surrogates?
4. What are the similarities and differences between defenses by Clinton and other political rhetors?

Chapter Two

The Theory of Image Restoration Discourse

Apologia has been studied using multiple methods, including Ware and Linkugel (1973) and Burke (1969). However, Benoit's (1995a) method, which integrates these diverse approaches, is the most comprehensive due to its expanded typology. This inclusive nature makes it a logical choice for application in this study.

Benoit's theory of image restoration has two major assumptions. First, it assumes that communication is a goal-oriented activity. Second, it assumes that the maintenance of a favorable image is one of the primary goals (Clark & Delia, 1979). With this understanding, the strategies for maintaining a good "face" can be addressed.

IMAGE REPAIR STRATEGIES

Benoit's (1995a) typology contains five major categories: denial, evading responsibility, reducing offensiveness, corrective action, and mortification. Additionally, three of these have subcategories, making a total of fourteen image repair strategies that rhetors choose to use. These are displayed in Table 2.1.

Denial

The denial category can be broken down into simple denial and shift the blame. In simple denial, a rhetor denies having done anything wrong. For example, a politician might insist, "I did not accept money from foreign industries."

Table 2.1
Image Restoration Strategies

Strategy	Key Characteristic	Example
Denial		
Simple Denial	did not perform act	I did not do it
Shift the blame	another performed act	My accountant did it
Evading Responsibility		
Provocation	response to another's act	Opponent attacked first
Defeasibility	lack of information/ability	Did not know about bill
Accident	mishap	Miscalculation was an accident
Good Intentions	meant well	Tried to reduce deficit
Reducing Offensiveness of Event		
Bolstering	stress good traits	Lood at accomplishments
Minimization	act not serious	Only twenty million
Differentiation	less offensive than similar acts	Not a tax increase, a revenue enhancer
Transcendence	more important values	Tax evasion as protest, not dishonesty
Attack Accuser	reduce accuser's credibility	Witness is a liar
Compensation	reimburse victim	Return illegal funds
Corrective Action	plan to solve/prevent recurrence of problem	New policy on accepting campaign contributions
Mortification	apologize	I'm very sorry

When shifting the blame, one attempts to lay responsibility for the transgression on another party. For instance, when charged with financial irregularities, an official might say, "My accountant was in charge of that transaction." In both of these examples, the accused tries to deny having done anything wrong.

Evading Responsibility

The evading responsibility category includes the sub-strategies of provocation, defeasibility, accident, and good intentions.

The provocation strategy is used when rhetors explain their behavior by claiming that the actions of another goaded them into the offensive behavior. For example, a politician accused of running negative advertisements could say, "My opponent attacked me first."

Rhetors may use the defeasibility strategy to indicate their lack of information or ability in a situation. For instance, a senator might claim he/she did not know about some harmful provision in a bill when voting for it.

A rhetor may try to evade responsibility for a misdeed by saying it was an accident. Consider the example of the congressional aid who miscalculated part of a budget initiative. The aid might say, "It was a mistake. The miscalculation was an accident." Thus, claiming a misdeed was accidental may be employed to restore a good image.

Finally, one may try to evade responsibility by claiming good intentions were behind the act. For instance, a president who raises taxes after promising not to might claim, "I wanted to lower the budget deficit. I thought it would help taxpayers." As such, claiming that good intentions prompted the misdeed can help restore a tarnished image.

Reducing the Offensiveness of an Event

An accused rhetor may also choose to maintain a favorable image by reducing the offensiveness of an event. This approach has six sub-strategies: bolstering, minimization, differentiation, transcendence, attack accuser, and compensation.

Bolstering involves reminding a particular audience of the accused person's many good qualities that should presumably make the current transgression less offensive. For instance, a president under attack for accepting illegal foreign money could ask that the public consider his/her otherwise excellent record in office. With so much accomplished, the indiscretion is presumably immaterial.

A rhetor uses minimization when he/she asks the audience to consider that the offense is minor in some way. For instance, a politician under attack for voting for an increased budget deficit might respond by saying, "It's only another twenty million dollars. That's a tiny portion of the budget." In this way, the rhetors seek to point out that the vote was less offensive than it appears at first glance.

Differentiation occurs when the accused attempts to define a deed as somehow different than what it has been called. For instance, a politician might say, "I did not raise taxes. I merely closed a few loopholes." In this instance, the politician wants the voter to think of this action as something other than a tax increase.

A rhetor may use transcendence to put the alleged misdeed in a larger context. For instance, a war protester might explain refusal to pay income tax by saying the offense was about peace, not greed. If this action can be placed in a larger context, the audience may not find it as offensive as simple tax evasion.

When accused of wrongdoing, rhetors may choose to attack their accusers. For instance, a senator who is accused of sexual harassment could call the accuser "a slut who knew what she was doing." In this instance, the accused not only shifts the focus away from his/her wrongdoing, but also attempts to reduce the offensiveness of the event by tying the accusation to some unworthy source.

Finally, one may choose to promise compensation for any misdeeds performed. For instance, when accused of accepting money from foreign governments, an official could choose to refund the money to the illegitimate source, making things right again. In this case, the politician sought to maintain a positive image by compensating for the wrongdoing.

Corrective Action

When a person, company, or other party is accused of wrongdoing, corrective action is another possibility for image repair. Where compensation involves some sort of payment or other in-kind arrangement, corrective action involves changing one's ways of conduct in order to prevent a recurrence. For example, the politician in the last example could articulate steps to be taken to avoid accepting illicit contributions, such as accepting money only from registered lobbyists. Corrective action is taken to prevent a recurrence of the misdeed.

Mortification

Finally, an accused party may decide to admit wrong-doing and express regret, or engage in mortification, over the episode in question. For instance, a politician who is convicted of drunk driving might apologize at length for that behavior and ask the constituents to forgive him/her for the foolish action.

PREVIOUS IMAGE RESTORATION RESEARCH

Benoit's (1995a) theory of image restoration strategies has been used to study persuasive defense in many contexts. This review of that research is divided into the genres of corporate, celebrity, political, and religious *apologia*. Each section reviews the applications chronologically.

Corporate *Apologia*

Benoit and Brinson (1994) examined the defense strategies used by AT&T after an extensive east coast telephone service interruption. AT&T executives first tried to shift the blame to lower-level employees, which was a strategy firmly rejected by the public. Next, they wisely decided to set in place procedures for guaranteeing reliable phone service in the future (corrective action).

Sellnow and Ulmer (1995) applied the method to crisis communication in the wake of Jack in the Box Restaurant's E. coli outbreak and subsequent deaths among its restaurant patrons. They asserted that Jack in the Box engaged in an effective combination of strategies: corrective action, which promised no future E. coli incidents; and compensation, through donations to charity and taking responsibility for victims' hospitalizations, which served to bolster the company's public image. Moreover, the company executives were highly accessible to the media, the public, and government officials. Sellnow and Ulmer found that these strategies led to "slow but consistent" recovery for the company (p. 149).

Benoit (1995a) examined the attacks and subsequent defenses of Coke and Pepsi colas in various exchanges in restaurant trade publications. Among the more serious charges were the assertions that Pepsi tasted better than Coke (as revealed in a taste test) and that Coke gave favorable treatment to McDonald's to the detriment of other fast-food chains. Simultaneously, Coke accused Pepsi of competing directly with its soft-drink customers (using its subsidiary fast-food chains) and of making false accusations against Coke.

Benoit determined that Coke's persuasive defense was superior to Pepsi's. Coke transcended when it pointed out that the better cola could be determined by unit sales rather than a taste test. Moreover, Coke's forceful denial of favoring McDonald's was well received and its image was bolstered by references to its market success. Coke also effectively attacked its accuser for making demonstrably false allegations.

Benoit (1995a) also studied Exxon's persuasive discourse following the Valdez oil spill in Alaska. He found that Exxon shifted the blame in two ways. First, the spill itself was blamed on Captain Joseph Hazelwood, who had been drinking and otherwise acting irresponsibly before the crash which caused the spill. Second, Exxon blamed the U.S. Coast Guard for delaying the cleanup of the spill.

Exxon engaged in minimization by downplaying the effects of the spill. It consistently claimed fewer numbers of animal corpses were found than did Alaska officials.

Exxon also attempted to bolster its image. The company began by praising its own actions subsequent to the spill, claiming the crisis was receiving Exxon's full attention, and finally, expressing sympathy for the local residents and people of Alaska.

Corrective action was employed as well. For instance, a policy of random drug and alcohol testing was implemented. Also, Exxon promised to do whatever was necessary to repair the damage.

Benoit concluded that Exxon's image repair was not effective, mostly because the inaction of its management in the wake of the crisis was so apparent. He argued that persuasive defense could not "be expected to work miracles" (p. 121). Public opinion polls revealed that the public viewed Exxon's responsibility for the spill negatively and that the vast majority of people thought the company could have done more to clean up the mess.

Union Carbide's persuasive defense following the notorious chemical accident in Bhopal, India, was also studied in Benoit (1995a). After a chemical cloud released into the air killed 2,000 and injured an additional 200,000, Union Carbide began its image repair with bolstering, expressing its shock and concern for the victims. Then, the company promised the corrective action of setting up a relief fund, opening an orphanage, and providing medical supplies and assistance.

Union Carbide attempted to shift the blame for its delay in releasing a public statement when it hinted that the arrest of the company chairman caused the delay. Finally, the company tried to differentiate itself as more of a volunteer offering service and aid rather than a guilty party forced to offer compensation.

Benoit claimed that Union Carbide's reliance on bolstering and corrective action were not enough to save its image from damage. He asserted that immediate expressions of mortification combined with plans to avoid future accidents would have been more appropriate. He also notes that the company may have benefited from "ethnocentrism," whereby the accident was not as damaging to the company's reputation as it would have been had the accident occurred in the United States.

Benoit (1995b) considered Sears' persuasive defense discourse after the company was accused of abusing its auto repair customers. The California Department of Consumer Affairs charged that Sears was routinely overcharging for services and performing unnecessary repairs. Sears' defense strategies included: denying any wrongdoing took place; differentiating the notion of "sales goals" with the "quotas" it was charged with imposing on its sales staffs; bolstering its image as a reputable American institution and the sales practices it used as an industry standard; claiming that the company's personnel acted only with good intentions; minimizing the misdeeds as being uncommon given the huge numbers of customers they dealt with; attacking the accuser, first for conducting a flawed investigation, and second for being politically motivated; and then promising corrective action, without ever offering regrets (mortification) over the matter. Benoit assessed this discourse as ineffective because of its lack of apology in the face of being so obviously guilty as charged.

Brinson and Benoit (1996) analyzed Dow Corning's defensive discourse after the company's silicon breast implants were found to be harmful. The image repair strategies came in three phases: phase one, simple denial; phase two, denial and reducing offensiveness; and phase three, mortification, corrective action, simple denial, and bolstering.

They discovered that Dow's initial chosen strategies of denying harmful effects in the implants and then distancing itself from the product were ineffective because the risky nature of the implants was discovered by the company's own researchers. The further attempts at hiding this discovery implied that the company was hiding something. The continued attacks against the company provided support for the public's disapproval of such behavior. They further found that once the company owned up to its responsibility and outlined details for guaranteeing the safety of future implant recipients, the attacks went into remission. In short, mortification and corrective action should have been the company's original strategies.

Benoit and Czerwinski (1997) studied USAir's image repair strategies in the wake of a crash near Pittsburgh. That company placed a series of persuasive defense advertisements in newspapers across the country. The company attempted to bolster its image by claiming how important travel safety was to the company and claiming its personnel are "professionals."

USAir also engaged in a subtle form of denial by ignoring the *New York Times'* charges that it had a history of safety violations. Finally, corrective action was offered in the form of an appointment of a former Air Force official to oversee safety and the selection of an aviation firm to audit its safety operations. Ultimately, Benoit and Czerwinski claimed these strategies were ineffective. The company's primary spokespeople, pilots, and flight attendants, all answered to company management and may have been perceived as interested parties. Moreover, that the ground crew did not write a letter on behalf of the company raised serious questions about safety maintenance. Finally, Benoit and Czerwinski said that the strategy of using independent experts to corroborate their accounts of the incident was never developed fully. All of these studies represent examples of how corporations might respond rhetorically when they come under attack for dishonesty, negligence, or any other disparaging quality.

Celebrity *Apologia*

Of course, preserving one's good reputation is not limited to a corporate domain. Benoit and Hanczor (1994) analyzed Olympic figure skater Tonya Harding's persuasive defense of her role in the assault on rival skater Nancy Kerrigan. They discovered that she bolstered her reputation in numerous ways, including references to her years of hard work and her unfortunate, abusive relationships with her mother and ex-husband. She engaged in denial by saying she had not violated the Olympic code of conduct, and that she had not known about the attack before it took place. On multiple occasions she attacked her primary accuser, ex-husband Jeff Gillooly. She also engaged in defeasibility when she claimed that she didn't go to the police immediately because the events transpired too quickly. Benoit and Hanczor evaluated her defense as ineffective due to the fact that she lied, claiming she had not known about the attack, which destroyed her credibility as a rhetor. She was also inconsistent in her statements. They cited negative public opinion polls to support their evaluation of her discourse's effectiveness.

Benoit and Anderson (1996) examined the persuasive defense of television character Murphy Brown following the infamous attack by Vice President Dan Quayle. Speaking in the Brown character, actress Candace Bergen engaged in simple denial, claiming that there was no glamorization of single motherhood on the show. The show also attacked Quayle, the accuser. Finally, Murphy's character was bolstered by references to her becoming maternal. Benoit and Anderson concluded that the response to the attack was generally effective, noting that her statements were augmented by characterizations on the show. For instance, her character was shown in an unglamorous situation, denying the glamorization charge; and single-parent families were shown to be thriving, supposedly refuting the two-parent necessity offered by Quayle. They also lauded the use of humor in the show as effective.

Benoit (1997) studied the defense strategies used by British actor Hugh Grant after his arrest for soliciting a prostitute. Grant engaged in mortification, bolstering, attack accuser, and denial in order to repair his image. Benoit evaluated the discourse favorably for a couple of major reasons. First, Grant appeared sincere in his mortification. Second, people tend to admire those who can admit to their mistakes. Benoit claims that the image repair could have been even better had Grant explicitly offered corrective action and admitted sorrow, which he did only implicitly. Benoit also argued that mortification might be a more amenable option for entertainers than for politicians or corporations, who might more likely be held to task by interested parties.

Political Image Repair

Recall from the previous review of presidential and other political *apologia* that Benoit, Gullifor, and Panici (1991) studied Reagan, Benoit (1995a) examined Nixon, and Kennedy and Benoit (1997) analyzed Gingrich. Benoit's (1995a) theory of image restoration strategies was employed for each of those studies.

Religious Image Repair

Blaney and Benoit (1997) examined Jesus Christ's use of persuasive defense in the Gospel according to John. They found that, when accused of unorthodoxy, Jesus engaged in transcendence in order to expand religious and moral consciousness. Also, he used the simple denial strategy to refute charges that were so damaging (blasphemy, for example) that his outright denial was necessary. They concluded that transcendence might be a natural strategy for religious rhetors whose interests tend to be otherworldly. This provides an example of defensive discourse among religious figures.

Other *Apologia* Applications

While Benoit's (1995a) method is the most comprehensive means for analyzing defensive discourse, other studies of *apologia* do exist. For instance, Huxman and Bruce (1995) examined the "distinct situational (accusatory), substantive (motivational), and stylistic (argumentative) factors that have never been viewed as dynamically interrelated" (p. 57) in the context of Dow Chemical Company's *apologia* during its production of napalm in the Vietnam War.

Hearit (1995) employed Ware and Linkugel's (1973) theory of *apologia* in viewing corporate and personal *apologia* as different genres, worthy of separate research programs. Examining the image repair of Exxon after the Alaskan oil spill and Domino's Pizza after several auto crash fatalities presumably related to their "30 minutes or free" policy for delivery, he finds that corporate *apologia* tends toward a dissociation with negative actions and a re-association with the public's values.

With Benoit's (1995a) method fully explained and the relevant scholarly literature reviewed, attention will turn to the specific plans of this study. The procedures are the topic of the next section.

HOW WE ANALYZED CLINTON'S IMAGE REPAIR

All of the studies cited above can provide exemplars for the application of Benoit's (1995a) method. However, the specific procedures used in this study are provided below.

As Ryan (1982) noted, in order to properly assess a rhetor's defense one must be well-acquainted with the attack (*kategoria*) which prompts the defense. This exchange of discourse is collectively known as the speech-set. The accusations against Clinton will come from myriad sources: newspaper clippings, wire services, press conferences, and television talk programs. Newspapers, magazines, talk show transcripts, and press conferences were searched in order to describe the accusations Clinton faced in each scandal.

Each scandal will be critically analyzed in a separate chapter. For each chapter there will be (1) a description of the accusations against Clinton, (2) an analysis of Clinton's (or a surrogate's) defense using Benoit's (1995a) typology, (3) an evaluation of that defense using criteria of internal consistency and plausibility, and (4) a discussion of external data supporting or disputing the evaluation. The evaluations will consider the particular audiences Clinton needed to persuade in each situation (e.g., primary voters, general election voters, etc.). After all of the applications have been completed, the theoretical contribution will be considered. Namely, the study will clarify (1) how various rhetorical situations impact the relative effectiveness of the strategies and (2) how defenses offered by surrogates can differ from those of the accused.

Defensive discourse following accusations that Clinton abused illegal drugs will include a composite of his chosen strategies assembled in a CNN *Special Report.* Defensive speech from the Whitewater affair will come from various statements made at press conferences presumably devoted to other issues where the media asked off-topic questions. Discourse in response to accusations of adultery with nightclub singer Gennifer Flowers will be transcribed from Bill and Hillary Clinton's January 26, 1992, interview on *60 Minutes.* Clinton's *apologia* following charges that he evaded the draft will come from his February 12, 1992, interview on ABC's *Nightline* program with Ted Koppel. Defensive discourse in the wake of the Monica Lewinsky matter will derive from January 21, 1998, interviews with PBS' *The News Hour* and *Roll Call* magazine as well as pertinent remarks following his January 26, 1998, address to an after-school program for children. Finally, the discourse used to examine image repair provided by surrogates will come from their respective White House press conferences and media appearances.

These texts were chosen because, in each case, they are the most substantial on record. Also, while the individual sets of discourse varied in their media prominence, each of the artifacts under consideration have been widely disseminated.

The external data used to assess the effectiveness of the various texts will include polling data related to Clinton's job approval and character approval. Additionally, editorials, columns, and all relevant letters to the editor of the *New York Times* will be considered. These commentaries will be used because they provide insight into the thoughts of opinion leaders (columnists and editorialists) and potential opinion leaders (letter writers). An incubation period of one week following the date of each image repair text will be allowed. In other words, data collected during the seven days following the image repair discourse will be used.

Chapter Three

To Serve or Not to Serve: Clinton's Draft Record

On February 12, 1992, Bill Clinton appeared on the ABC television program *Nightline* with host Ted Koppel to discuss the matter of Clinton's unconventional draft record. A February 6, 1992, *Wall Street Journal* article scrutinizing events surrounding his draft situation prompted questions about his ability to act as commander-in-chief of the U.S. armed forces. In this chapter, the allegations made in that article will be explained, followed by an analysis of image restoration strategies Clinton used in the aftermath. Finally, an evaluation of the effectiveness of Clinton's discourse will be offered.

THE PERSUASIVE ATTACK

The *Wall Street Journal* article by Jeffrey Birnbaum revealed that on August 7, 1969, Clinton was offered a draft deferment (classified as 1–D) for promising to enroll in the Army ROTC program at the University of Arkansas. That same month, he returned to his graduate studies as a Rhodes Scholar at Oxford University in England. On September 19, 1969, President Nixon announced a cutback in the number of people drafted from October to December, the months when Clinton was likely to be drafted under the old system had he not attained a deferment. On October 30, 1969, Clinton was reclassified as eligible for the draft when the ROTC program at Arkansas informed the local draft board that Clinton would not be enrolling. On November 26, 1969, Congress passed the lottery law which mandated that new draftees be determined by the chance drawing of birthdates. On December 1, Clinton's birthdate was given a draft lottery number that was too high to be called into duty. The next day he applied to Yale Law School and the day after that Clinton wrote U.S. Army Coronel Eugene Holmes (the ROTC recruiter), thanking him for "saving me [Clinton] from the draft" (Balz and Broder, 1992, p. A1).

Birnbaum's (1992) *Wall Street Journal* report revealed that Clinton never applied to the University of Arkansas, which challenged Clinton's assertion that he wished to train in ROTC. Clinton's mother, Virginia Kelley, confirmed that she believed Clinton never intended to attend Arkansas.

At face value, it appeared that Clinton, facing likely conscription, asked for an ROTC deferment, which he accepted and then reneged upon, after learning of his better chances of being passed over for the draft. Mary McGrory (1992) quoted Nebraska Senator and Clinton's Democratic rival, Robert Kerrey, saying that Clinton's explanation of his draft record "does not have the ring of truth" (p. A2). Other Democrats, hopeful that Clinton might have the potential to take back the White House, feared that his candidacy "could fall apart at any moment . . . over his draft deferment" (Edsall, 1992a, p. A8). As a candidate running for the office of commander-in-chief of the military, his image was certainly in peril. Klein (1992) asserted that his campaign had been dragged down by the allegations. Clinton needed to address five charges: (1) that he had violated draft laws, (2) that he had acted opportunistically to evade the draft, (3) that he had changed his account of the events surrounding his draft history, (4) that he lacked the credibility and patriotism to be commander-in-chief of the U.S. Armed Forces, and (5) that the allegations had damaged his candidacy.

THE PERSUASIVE DEFENSE

An analysis of Clinton's appearance on *Nightline* reveals that he used eight strategies for image restoration. He relied primarily on denial and bolstering, but also used defeasibility, transcendence, differentiation, good intentions, minimization, and attack accuser. The individual strategies will be discussed in that order.

Denial

One could argue that a candidate for president of the United States invariably must avoid being perceived as cowardly or unpatriotic. For this reason, Clinton's use of denial is not unexpected.

Asked if his slip in the New Hampshire polls could be attributed to the *Wall Street Journal* story, Clinton made an assertive denial:

The *Journal* story itself confirmed what I said all along, which is that I gave up my deferment before the lottery came in, I was in the draft. It was the luck of the draw that I got a high lottery number. I did not dodge the draft, I did not do anything wrong, and that has not been contradicted, even by people who have changed their stories over the intervening years. (*Nightline,* February 12, 1992)

This statement actually provided two denials. First, he denied that he was being deferred at the time of the draft and asserted that he was indeed in the draft. Second, he denied avoiding the draft. This two-part denial was repeated again: "I was in the draft before the lottery came in. I gave up the deferment. I got a high lottery number and I wasn't called. That's what the records reflect" (*Nightline,* February 12, 1992). In these instances, the main denial was basically that no irregularities occurred in his draft situation.

With the larger denials out of the way, Clinton pressed on with denials about peculiarities in the sequence of his draft record. Koppel, noting that Clinton applied to Yale Law School the day after the draft lottery, and wrote the letter to Colonel Holmes the day after that, opined: "There does seem to be a sense about those two actions of someone who knew, or at least was fairly confident at that point, that he was not going to be drafted" (*Nightline,* February 12, 1992). Clinton denied this interpretation:

Well, I don't think that's right. I can remember, even up in the spring, as late as March of the next year, being told that I might not be able to do anything else, that I might be called in that year. We didn't know for some time that we would not be called for sure.... I remember distinctly being told at some point after that, we checked at home and I was told that they couldn't say with any certainty that I could do anything other than spend another term at Oxford, that I might—I'd probably be able to stay through May, but that's all I knew. (*Nightline,* February 12, 1992)

His denial of acting opportunistically continued when Koppel again asked if the sequence of dates and actions could be merely coincidental:

There's nothing to read into it. The important thing for the American people to know is that in late September, early October, sometime about that time, I think it was in September, I had talked to my stepfather, I asked him to talk to the draft board and to Colonel Holmes, asked that I be put back into the draft. I was put into the draft before the lottery came along, before I knew my lottery number, and I was in the draft. (*Nightline,* February 12, 1992)

In these statements, Clinton denied specifically that he knew he would not be drafted. He took great care to indicate that he had no idea what might happen with his draft status. If this were true, then he could not be accused of engaging in a cynical form of draft evasion.

Finally, Clinton summarized his previous statements, saying, "So the bottom line is, I wasn't a draft-dodger." If the public believed his version of the events, then an effective denial of draft-dodging had been made.

Bolstering

There were several instances of bolstering in Clinton's discourse, each designed to focus on Clinton's accomplishments or character traits that could mitigate any appearance of wrongdoing during his draft eligibility period. In the first instance, Clinton addressed Koppel's question about how a campaign so damaged (going from the front of the pack in New Hampshire to well behind Paul Tsongas in the polls) by allegations of draft-dodging can rebound:

Frankly, I've been amazed at the number of my supporters in New Hampshire and the number of people who've stayed with us. I mean, after all, they just met me a few months ago, they don't know much about me. It's not like they've worked through eleven years of hard issues and all the things I've done as governor. They've not seen the real evidence of my political leadership and character, and so I think they've had all this stuff dumped on them here in the last two or three weeks, and finally the dam broke and they're asking themselves questions. The encouraging thing, to me, is looking into the eyes of the voters with whom I'm shaking hands and going to these meetings where we're still drawing very, very large crowds, is that I think people are going to take another look. (*Nightline,* February 12, 1992)

This instance of bolstering served two major functions. First, it asserted that his campaign was still viable and strong. Second, it allowed Clinton the opportunity to explain why his support would stay with him, for example, his record as governor. By talking about his "political leadership and character" he bolstered his candidacy in the face of the allegations.

He bolstered again: "I feel good about what happened today, I feel good about yesterday, and I'm going to fight like crazy from here on in" (*Night-*

line, February 12, 1992). Again, Clinton underscored the quality of his support in spite of the scandal and, when he promised to "fight like crazy," he bolstered his personal tenacity, which is a quality many look for in a leader.

When Koppel's questioning shifted to how Clinton might hypothetically deal with selective draft resistance (as opposed to conscientious objection) among young men if his administration needed a draft implemented, Clinton bolstered himself again: "Well, first of all, in a democracy I favor the kind of volunteer force that we have now. If we had had a draft, then I would have gone to Congress and asked for an explicit declaration of war" (*Nightline,* February 12, 1992). In this statement, Clinton spoke of his ideal military situation: a volunteer army unless war had been declared. This line of reasoning allowed him to portray himself as responsible on the defense issue despite his resistance to military service in the late 1960s.

Clinton pointed to his virtues again by asserting that he had always been forthcoming about the issue:

> And let me say this, Ted. Back in 1978, when this was first raised, I had not seen or heard from Colonel Holmes for nine years. We'd had no contact. The minute someone asked me about it, I said, "Call Colonel Holmes." I didn't talk to any handlers. I didn't run around and think about anything, I just said, "Call him." (*Nightline,* February 12, 1992)

In this passage, Clinton attempted to point to his above-the-board handling of the issue in previous campaigns as evidence of his honesty in dealing with this issue. When he told the press to "call Colonel Holmes," he implied that he had nothing to hide. This probably served as testimony to his forthcoming nature.

Clinton also bolstered himself as a patriot when he talked about the content of the infamous letter: "At least I was involved in the issues of my time, I cared deeply about them. That's the way I feel." This caring about the social upheaval circa 1969 is offered as evidence of his concern for America. His patriotism, he would argue, could be seen in his political participation against what he thought was an unjust war. He expressed further patriotic sentiments:

> One of the most precious memories of my childhood is my mother trying to get me to know my dead father, showing me a presidential citation, some sort of citation he'd received for good duty in the war. I was proud of that. I wanted to be part of my country's defense and my

country's service. Then I turned against the Vietnam War. I hated doing that. It was an anguishing thing for me. You can tell that from the
letter. (*Nightline,* February 12, 1992)

With these words, Clinton portrayed himself as inherently patriotic and
pro-American, which could allay some of the negativity associated with his
draft record. One could argue that the above represented transcendence by
calling the justice of the Vietnam War into question. However, this discourse was aimed at persuading the audience that he was sufficiently patriotic to be commander-in-chief. As such, the passage should be interpreted
as bolstering his patriotism.

Next, he asserted that he had the competence and sympathies necessary
for military administration:

Then I became governor, commander of my National Guard. I've
called out the guard to quell a riot at Fort Chaffee. I supported the National Guard and the veterans' groups of my state strongly. I supported
our involvement in the Persian Gulf War. I have no doubt about my ca-
pacity to be commander-in-chief. (*Nightline,* February 12, 1992)

By pointing to his experience with the Arkansas National Guard, Clinton
bolstered his perception as militarily competent and responsive. This could
be important in light of the draft-dodging allegations.

Finally, Clinton asked the *Nightline* audience blatantly to consider his
accomplishments: "If we're going to talk about twenty-two years ago, let's
talk about my whole record as governor, my demonstrations of character,
my fitness to lead" (*Nightline,* February 12, 1992). Here, he advanced the
argument that if one is considering his actions of long ago, one should also
consider the good he accomplished as governor of Arkansas.

Defeasibility

Clinton also attempted to argue that the situation was out of his control
on multiple occasions. Asked whether the allegations could explain his dip
in the New Hampshire polls, Clinton explained:

I was home trying to get over the flu, and there were a lot of press reports over the weekend saying, "Well, this raises questions about his
electability and questions about character," and I think a lot of people
heard from it secondhand. I should have put an ad on right away, as
soon as the story broke. (*Nightline,* February 12, 1992)

In this statement, Clinton implies that the poll numbers dropped because he was physically ill, not because he was unfit for office because of the draft allegations. As such, the circumstances in which he lost ground were beyond his control.

Another example of defeasibility came in response to Koppel's question:

You initially told reporters that you weren't aware of the fact that you had a high number in the lottery, then later on you told my colleague Jim Wooten that you probably did know. Which was it? Have you refreshed your memory on it?

To which Clinton replied:

I honestly don't remember, but I think that in this day and age of instantaneous communications most people would find it difficult to believe that I did not know. I don't know whether I knew or not . . . I just don't know. (*Nightline,* February 12, 1992)

In this instance Clinton argued that he lacked the ability needed to answer the question. He also had memory problems when asked if the series of events in 1969 did not seem too coincidental: "I say, I just don't remember" (*Nightline,* February 12, 1992). His memory had failed him.

He used defeasibility again in reference to his Yale Law School application, which was made the day after he was assigned a high draft number: "I was in the draft, and so I was going to be called or go to law school, and I didn't know for sure then" (*Nightline,* February 12, 1992). Here, the point he made was that he did not know what was going to happen with his draft status so he applied to law school.

Finally, he defended the contents of the letter to Col. Holmes: "Well, let's look at it. First of all, it is the letter of a deeply agitated 23–year-old boy, a young man" (*Nightline,* February 12, 1992). In other words, he could not be held responsible for those actions since he was too young to behave prudently at the time.

Differentiation

Clinton also used differentiation to describe events as being different from what they appeared to be at first glance. For instance, Koppel pressed Clinton further on whether it was permissible for young men to object to particular wars:

The way things are right now, I should explain to our audience, is you're either a conscientious objector across the board, you can't pick and choose, you can't say, "I like this war," "I don't like that war." Where does Bill Clinton stand on that issue today? (*Nightline,* February 12, 1992)

To this Clinton replied:

I have somewhat different feelings about that now. I think we ought to have a draft only when there is clear and present need, when we're going to have a lot of people in harm's way, when the volunteer army is insufficient to the task, and when there ought to be broad-based service. I do think when you have a general draft, at least there ought to be a declaration of war, so that Congress can say the broad national interests are at issue, or at least something like Senator Nunn's War Powers Act ought to be enacted. (*Nightline,* February 12, 1992)

Here, Clinton attempted to differentiate selective objection to war, which he had ascribed to during Vietnam, with what he would tolerate as commander-in-chief. He argued that under his administration, selective objection would not be an issue because his mode of military action would be different. There would only be a draft when it was really needed and when war had been officially declared by the elected Congress. As such, Clinton said he would not be in a position where he would have to confront selective objectors.

When asked what he would have done about selective objectors had he been president in 1969, he responded:

Well, I would have asked the Congress for an explicit expression of support through the United Nations, and I think I would have asked, if we'd had the draft, I would have asked them to actually declare war. I think once the Congress declares war under the Constitution, then you can have a broad conscription. . . . I think it was warranted in World War II. I think, as I said, I supported the conflict in Korea. Our country has shown over and over again that large numbers of our people will voluntarily serve in the armed forces when there is broad-based support for a policy, when they understand it. That was clearly the case in Desert Storm. (*Nightline,* February 12, 1992)

This answer served to differentiate the Vietnam situation from any military situation he would oversee as chief executive. Any conscription in his administration would be due to a widely popular, officially declared war. Such a scenario was in stark contrast to the Vietnam policy, which was an unpopular police action initiated and maintained through the executive branch. This differentiation was underscored again: "If we had had a draft, then I would have gone to Congress and asked for an explicit declaration of war, then I would not have approved of selective conscientious objection" (*Nightline,* February 12, 1992). Thus, Clinton answered questions about how he would deal with draft resisters as commander-in-chief by differentiating any draft policy he would implement with the draft policy of the Vietnam era. This answer allowed him to argue that he still had the moral authority to activate troops and implement a military conscription if the need were presented. Notably, Clinton differentiated the Vietnam episode with any hypothetical situation he might have as commander-in-chief on two grounds: any draft under his supervision would be the consequence of (1) an officially declared war with (2) widespread public support.

Another example of differentiation addressed the very important issue of whether Clinton had opportunistically resigned his ROTC deferment only after learning of the draft lottery. Clinton insisted that he had a more noble motivation for giving up the deferment: "I didn't think it right to have a four-year deferment and I ought to go back into the draft" (*Nightline,* February 12, 1992). One could argue that he was claiming he had good intentions. However, in this context, he was addressing the issue of whether his actions were opportunistic. Indeed, he was differentiating the honorable and patriotic from the cowardly and despicable.

Transcendence

Clinton also employed transcendence on multiple occasions. For instance, in discussing the prominence of the draft-dodging allegations in his chances for winning the New Hampshire primary, he asserted:

> The people in this state are fundamentally fair, they're hurting, they desperately want this election to be about their tomorrows, their future, their problems, not about my yesterdays. (*Nightline,* February 12, 1992)

In this statement, Clinton attempted to place the allegations in a much larger context. In other words, he claimed that the voters would ultimately decide that the election should have more to do with the problems and future needs of New Hampshire and the whole country than the details of Clinton's past.

The strategy was employed again when Clinton tried to set an agenda for what mattered in the campaign: "When you hear all the static, one way or the other, what only matters when you strip it all away is who can lead this country to greatness" (*Nightline,* February 12, 1992). In other words, Clinton argued that the discussion of the allegations was "static," mere distraction from what was really important. As such, his draft history was transcended by his vision for leading our country to greatness.

Clinton also focused on the irrelevance of the issue when placed in temporal context: "We've been talking about a letter I wrote 22 years ago as if it's a test of present presidential character" (*Nightline,* February 12, 1992). This statement implied that the time period involved (22 years ago) made the issue inconsequential to the issue of presidential character. The implication was that the election was about things much more important than a letter written many years before.

Finally, Clinton used transcendence to discuss the status of his candidacy. When assessing the presidential contenders, New Hampshire voters should

> look for a person with a vision, with a plan, with a record, and with a capacity to change their lives for the better. I'm going to try to give this election back to the people, to lift the cloud off of this election. For three weeks, of course, I've had some problems in the polls. All I've been asked about by the press are a woman I didn't sleep with and a draft I didn't dodge. Now I'm going to try to give them this election back, and if I can give it back to them and fight for them and their future, I think we've got a chance to do well here and I know we can go beyond here and continue to take this fight to the American people. (*Nightline,* February 12, 1992)

In other words, Clinton asserted that the futures of New Hampshirites was most important, more so than any allegations of adultery or draft-dodging. Furthermore, he implied, unless the focus of the election returned to the candidate's "vision," then democracy itself was imperiled. When Clinton claimed he wanted to "give them this election back" he argued that he wanted to put the focus on New Hampshirites and their problems and future rather than on him and his past.

Good Intentions

Only one instance of claiming good intentions was found in the program. The letter to Colonel Holmes, Clinton claimed "is a true reflection of the deep and conflicted feelings of a just-turned-23–year-old young man. I felt that at the time" (*Nightline,* February 12, 1992). Clearly, Clinton attempted to portray the contents of the letter as coming from someone who was sincerely trying to do what was right. One could argue that this represented bolstering of an idealistic youth. However, the issue at hand is the action he took in writing the letter and his belief that he was being virtuous at the time for writing it. Clearly, he claimed that he intended to do the right thing.

Minimization

On one occasion Clinton chose to minimize his actions by claiming that they were relatively minor issues:

The fact that I didn't serve after putting myself in the lottery should not be disabling. I mean, Dick Cheney, the Secretary of Defense, had deferments all the way through. I didn't have deferments all the way through. But I think he's been a pretty good secretary of defense. (*Nightline,* February 12, 1992)

Clearly, the argument advanced in this statement was that Dick Cheney, current Secretary of Defense, had a draft deferment through the whole period and still did a good job as secretary. On the other hand, Clinton gave up a deferment (presumably making him less a dodger than Cheney) and therefore, could do a good job as well. In short, what Clinton did was minimal compared to others who have been in charge of the country's defense.

Attack Accuser

Clinton also attacked his opponent, President George Bush. Notably, Clinton's primary accusers were other Democrats like Senator Kerrey, whom Clinton was running against. However, it is not surprising that Clinton would attack the likely Republican nominee as well. Indeed, Bush would ultimately be the opponent and would most surely exploit Clinton's draft irregularities. As a mode of self-defense, Clinton attacked Bush:

Twenty-two days ago, George Bush gave a State of the Union address, promised a tax cut for the middle class and capital gains for the wealthy. Today, 22 days later, he's up here in New Hampshire, where people are hurting, where the Food Stamp and welfare and unemployment rolls have tripled, and he says, "Well we're going to put off this

middle-class tax cut, but I want a bigger cut for the wealthy." I think
that's a test of presidential character. (*Nightline,* February 12, 1992)

In short, Clinton attacked Bush for allegedly not doing what he had proposed just days before. The fact that he was in New Hampshire, where the
middle class had economic problems, talking about tax cuts for the rich
made Bush's tax policies all the worse according to Clinton. This attack
served to point the public's attention to George Bush's character.

EVALUATION

This discourse will be evaluated by two criteria. First, it will be considered whether Clinton's image repair attempts were internally consistent
and plausible. Second, external evidence will be considered to assess the effectiveness of the discourse.

Internal Consistency and Plausibility

If one does not want to be perceived as a draft-dodger, it would make
sense to deny being one. Clinton denied this charge directly. He also denied
that the *Wall Street Journal* provided any revelation of things he had not
said before. In effect, his denials covered (1) doing anything wrong and (2)
changing his account of the events. One could argue that denial of
draft-dodging was absolutely essential in order to maintain credibility as a
candidate for commander-in-chief.

It is perfectly reasonable for someone under attack for a particular incident to point to past accomplishments in order to bolster one's image. As
such, Clinton pointed to his record as governor of Arkansas, including his
command of the Arkansas National Guard. He spoke of his many years of
working on hard issues and his political character in dealing with those issues. This was necessary to counter any perceived deficiencies of character
or competence brought on by the allegations.

Clinton adeptly handled the question of why his polling numbers had
suffered following the allegations. When he claimed that his lackluster response to the charge was due to his bout with the flu, he argued that the situation was beyond his control. Since most people have had such illnesses
where their productivity waned, the excuse was relatable to the voters. As
such, defeasibility was an appropriate choice.

Clinton's use of transcendence was artful as well. While he maintained
all along that he had done nothing wrong, his argument that the election
should concern economic issues probably resonated with New Hampshire

voters, who were living in the epicenter of the New England recession. Benoit and Wells (1998) found that three criteria enhance a political candidate's transcendence: (1) the issues an accused claims to be neglecting must be more important than the charges against the accused, (2) the accused must be perceived as distracted by the charges, and (3) the audience must perceive the accused as capable of addressing the neglected issues. Arguably, Clinton met all three criteria. The New Hampshire voters Clinton was trying to persuade were mired in the brutal New England recession of 1991–92. One could easily conclude that they were more interested in their economic solutions than Clinton's youthful foolery. He finished second in the primary to Paul Tsongas, from the neighboring state of Massachusetts. As such, one could argue that New Hampshirites believed he could address the substantive issues of the campaign. As far as perceived distraction from the issues, New Hampshirites doubtlessly saw that Clinton was forced to deal with the accusations on *Nightline* and in other forms. In short, Clinton's use of transcendence met all three criteria.

Clinton used differentiation effectively. The question of how he would deal with selective objectors as president was a sticky one, since he appeared to have tried to avoid service in a particular war with which he disagreed, but which may have left his patriotism in doubt. However, he made the case that Vietnam was a unique situation because it involved conscription of unwilling men into an undeclared, unpopular war. There would be no such problems in his administration because he would only activate a draft under more favorable conditions.

Claiming one had good intentions can be, but isn't automatically, an effective way of evading responsibility for a misdeed. Again, while denying any wrongdoing, Clinton maintained that the letter he wrote came from the depths of his sincerity. In effect, his argument claimed: "I didn't do anything wrong, but what I did do had good intentions." As such, his audience might be less judgmental about the contents of the letter. Moreover, the underscoring of his youth added to the argument that the letter was the result of a naive idealism.

Clinton used the minimization strategy well when he compared his draft record with that of Defense Secretary Cheney. While Cheney, apparently an excellent defense official, had a deferment through his whole period of eligibility, Clinton's deferment was shorter and ultimately given up to be part of the draft. As such, Clinton's use of deferment was minimal compared to Cheney's. Moreover, since Cheney performed honorably in spite of his deferment, there was no reason why Clinton should be perceived as incapable of performing military functions.

Finally, Clinton's attack on George Bush was effective. It mitigated the damage to Clinton's reputation by calling the current commander-in-chief's character into question. In this sense, it was appropriate for Clinton to attack his eventual opponent so that the charges from that source would be less damning during the general election.

Analysis of Clinton's discourse indicates that his choices of strategies were plausible and internally consistent. Polling data and public commentary support this evaluation.

Polling Data

Polling data from the days before and after Clinton's *Nightline* appearance support the claim that his overall image repair was at least somewhat, if not wholly, successful. A Gallup (1992) poll conducted February 4–6, 1992, showed that Democratic voters preferred Clinton (37 percent), who was followed by former Massachusetts Senator Paul Tsongas (24 percent), Nebraska Senator Bob Kerrey (12 percent), former California Governor Jerry Brown (8 percent), and Iowa Senator Tom Harkin (8 percent). Only days later, just following the *Wall Street Journal* article exposing the allegations, Clinton's lead evaporated. By the February 11–13 polling period, Tsongas led among Democratic voters by a 37 percent to 22 percent margin. Moreover, Clinton's Democratic favorability rating dropped abruptly from 73 percent during the February 4–6 period to 61 percent during the February 11–13 period. As such, one could argue that the draft allegations did substantial harm to Clinton's candidacy.

However, he managed a sizable rebound following the *Nightline* appearance. He made a respectable showing in New Hampshire, losing by a 29 percent to 22 percent margin to Tsongas, who was from the neighboring New England state of Massachusetts. A seven point loss under these conditions could be considered successful.

In the end, Clinton's proposition that New Hampshire voters would base their decisions on "their future, their problems, not about my yesterdays," (*Nightline*, February 12, 1992) may have been accurate. A Gallup (1992) report found that 78 percent of the voters were either ambivalent or more likely to vote for Clinton based on the draft allegations and the way he handled the charges. Only 20 percent of those polled said they were less likely to vote for Clinton. This data lends support to a positive evaluation for Clinton's image repair.

Commentary

Additionally, some commentary and letters to the editor in the *New York Times* support this assessment. An editorial opined:

On present evidence, Bill Clinton worked to avoid the draft, at times cleverly, but in ways that accorded with accepted common practice among others of his generation. Against that history, this Vietnam echo looks like an irrelevance that ought not distract New Hampshire voters from judging Bill Clinton on his merits. (Bill Clinton's Vietnam Test, February 14, 1992, p. A28)

In other words, the Times' editorial staff subscribed to Clinton's transcendence argument—that the draft issue was unimportant to current events and should not be important to voters.

Referring to the letter in question, columnist Anna Quindlen's (1992a) assessment was even more favorable:

It is an intelligent and eloquent letter, and it has made admirers of some who were not so sure of Mr. Clinton before. I would have been proud to have raised a child capable of writing it. It describes my own belief: that the war was a senseless waste. (p. E15)

According to this view, the letter was described not as manipulative or cynical, but as a great moral deed.

Author Elizabeth Becker (1992) added to the president's defense:

To decide that Governor Clinton is no longer Presidential material because he avoided the draft and opposed the war is to admit that America feels guilty about Vietnam . . . as his letter attests, he took the war seriously. It is a confession, alternating between high moral conviction and the raw ambitions of a politician. He mentions how tortured he and his friends were about the war. This is not a coward's note; it reflects angst. (p. A29)

In short, Becker asked readers to see Clinton's draft status as a way of looking at our long-term beliefs about the war. The fact that Clinton's record bothered people, she argued, had less to do with his ability to be president than our inability to come to grips with the darkness of that period. She echoed Clinton's transcendence argument insofar as she held that his Vietnam status was unimportant to presidential qualifications.

Not all of the *New York Times* commentary was favorable. International relations professor Walter McDougall's (1992) disgust with the situation was blatant:

> Much of the press wants to pardon Mr. Clinton since what he did to avoid the draft was accepted practice among his generation. But the moral philosophy behind that brief is not credible. Responsible adults don't allow their own teen-agers to peddle the dodge that "everyone's doing it." Nor is Governor Clinton "everyone," but a candidate for President. Nor is the behavior of my 60's generation the most laudable standard for civic deportment. Nor can Mr. Clinton plead youthful ill judgment, for his letter makes clear that he knew precisely what he was doing. He wanted to have it both ways: to make no sacrifice and pay no future price. (p. A27)

This passage indicated contempt for the idea that Clinton's offense should be forgiven because of the prevailing practices of the time. He continued his disdain:

> The man who dodges the draft cheats on us all, on the Republic. Mr. Clinton aspires to govern. The point is not that he protested the war—the war was a folly, in means if not motives. The point is not that civil disobedience is wrong—it often reflects a higher patriotism. The point is that Mr. Clinton arranged matters so to "avoid both Vietnam and the resistance." (p. A27)

In other words, Clinton's "agonizing" over the war was not sincere because he could have enlisted or resisted (honorably, either way), but chose to manipulate the system instead. This author would also raise another issue which casts doubt on his sincerity. The fact that Clinton tried to obtain Army and Air Force officer candidate school admission proved that he was not so much against participation in the war as he was against being a "grunt" enlisted man. Officer candidate school graduates would have been activated immediately. With this in mind, one could conclude that Clinton was trying to avoid trench combat more than anything else.

CONCLUSION

The analysis of Clinton's February 12, 1992, appearance on ABC's *Nightline* program illustrated that Clinton's primary defenses were denial and bolstering. However, he also used defeasibility, transcendence, differentiation, good intentions, minimization, and attack accuser. His discourse was generally successful in repairing his image, which was initially damaged by allegations of draft-dodging. While he could not expect to persuade everyone, he managed to remain a viable candidate who was near the front of the pack.

Chapter Four

"Pain in My Marriage":
Gennifer Flowers and Infidelity

On January 26, 1992, Bill and Hillary Clinton appeared on the CBS newsmagazine *60 Minutes* in an interview with reporter Steve Kroft. The subject was Clinton's alleged marital infidelity with nightclub singer and former Arkansas state employee Gennifer Flowers. In this chapter, the allegations will be explained, Clinton's discourse will be applied using Benoit's (1995a) method, and finally, the discourse will be evaluated for its effectiveness.

THE PERSUASIVE ATTACK

The infamous allegations against Clinton were rather sordid in their origins. Former nightclub singer and Arkansas employee Gennifer Flowers alleged in a paid interview with the *Star* gossip tabloid that she had a twelve–year love affair with Clinton when he was governor of Arkansas. This allegation might not have been as threatening to Clinton's candidacy had the story remained on the margins of credibility. However, as Kroft (*60 Minutes*, 1992) noted during the introduction to the Clinton interview, the mainstream press printed the story as well. Because committing adultery is a violation of the Ten Commandments, which many Americans hold in esteem, the charge was potentially quite damaging to Clinton's character and candidacy. *Washington Post* columnist Howard Kurtz (1992) reported that Clinton lost 12 points in the New Hampshire poll subsequent to the allegations of adultery. Kurtz also described Clinton as "under siege over allegations involving his marital fidelity" (Kurtz, 1992, p. A18). Steve Roberts

(1992) quoted an anonymous Democratic insider: "If he can't handle this, how could he handle a Kuwait?"(p. 30). In short, Clinton had to demonstrate his ability to deal with this allegation. Clinton needed image repair. The accusers in this case were two-fold: Flowers, the source of the allegations; and the news media, the public purveyors of the charges. He needed to address two accusations: (1) that he had committed adultery and (2) that his infidelity disqualified him as a presidential candidate.

THE PERSUASIVE DEFENSE

On January 26, 1992, immediately following the Super Bowl (television's largest assembled audience) on CBS, Bill and Hillary appeared on the program *60 Minutes.* Notably, this interview was just days before the February New Hampshire Democratic primary. During the interview, Clinton engaged in five strategies: denial, bolstering, attack accuser, transcendence, and differentiation. They will be discussed in that order.

Denial

Of all of the strategies, Clinton relied on denial most heavily. Some of the denials were quite explicit while others were implicit.

An example of an explicit denial can be seen in Clinton's answer to Kroft's probe about Flowers' allegation of a twelve–year affair: "It—that allegation is false" (*60 Minutes,* January 26, 1992). Here, Clinton made a direct rebuttal, declaring that what was alleged was simply not true. However, this was the only direct, forceful, and explicit denial of the charges of adultery. The other denials were all implicit and rather carefully worded.

For instance, when asked if he categorically denied ever having an affair with Flowers, he offered: "I've said that before and so has she" (*60 Minutes,* January 26, 1992). In other words, he did not repeat a denial verbatim such as, "Yes, I categorically deny having ever had an affair with Miss Flowers." Rather, he pointed to the fact that he had made such a denial in the past.

Clinton made another implicit denial when asked to describe his relationship with Miss Flowers:

Very limited, but until this, you know, friendly, but limited. I have—I met her in the late '70s when I was attorney general. She was one of a number of young people who were working for the television stations around Little Rock. And people in politics and the people in the media knew each other then, just as they do now. She left our state, and for years I didn't really hear from her or know what she was doing. Then she came back—I don't know—some time a few years ago and went to work again in the state. So that's how—that's who she is. (*60 Minutes,* January 26, 1992)

In this statement, Clinton implied a few denials. First, by describing the relationship as "friendly, but limited," Clinton implied there was no romance, only friendship. Second, he explained that their contacts were professionally driven: "She was one of a number of young people who were working for the television stations around Little Rock. And people in politics and people in the media knew each other then, just as they do now" (*60 Minutes,* January 26, 1992). As such, Clinton described the relationship as quite normal for the circumstances, not unusual or clandestine. Such a description may have helped explain how the two came to know each other, a question some voters may have been curious about.

Third, Clinton claimed that Flowers had left Arkansas and that he "didn't really hear from her or know what she was doing" (*60 Minutes,* January 26, 1992). Clearly, such an assertion supports his denial, because such a scenario would have made a twelve–year affair temporally impossible.

Just seconds later, Clinton continued with a series of denials. He used Flowers' alleged words to deny: "When this story—this rumor story got started in the middle of 1980 and she was contacted and told about it, she was so upset, and she called back and she said 'How could I be listed on this?'" (*60 Minutes,* January 26, 1992). In other words, the alleged affair was a "rumor," which is not necessarily true. Next in the series, Clinton used Flowers' alleged words to him in order to make an implied denial: "I haven't seen you for more than ten minutes in ten years" (*60 Minutes,* January 26, 1992). This statement added to the case for denial by hinting at the improbability that the affair could have physically taken place.

Yet another statement in this series implied a denial:

She would call from time to time when she was upset . . . and I would call her back—either she would call the office or I would call her back there at the office or I would call her back at the house, and Hillary knew when I was calling her back. I think once I called her when we were together. And so there's nothing out of the ordinary there. (*60 Minutes,* 1992)

Here, the denial was implied when Clinton claimed Hillary knew about the phone calls exchanged between Flowers and himself. Surely, no man would carry on an illicit affair with his wife's knowledge. Also, by insisting that there was "nothing out of the ordinary," one might conclude that this meant no romance had occurred.

Having examined Clinton's use of denial, one should note that he denied the affair with Flowers both implicitly and explicitly. He also used Flowers' alleged words to reinforce his denial.

Bolstering

Clinton also bolstered his image in the wake of the allegations. Responding to Kroft's skepticism over Clinton's candor, Clinton stated:

> Look, Steve, you go back and listen to what I've said. You know, I have acknowledged wrongdoing, I have acknowledged causing pain in my marriage. I have said things to you tonight and to the American people from the beginning that no American politician ever has. (*60 Minutes,* January 26, 1992)

This statement bolstered his image by arguing that he had been *more* forthcoming than most politicians, which should presumably be a positive character trait. He also implied that politicians in the past simply did not say much regarding these matters. In short, Clinton argued that he was setting a positive precedent.

He bolstered his candidness again: "I think most Americans who are watching this tonight, they'll know what we're saying, they'll get it, and they'll feel that we have been more candid" (*60 Minutes,* January 26, 1992). In short, Clinton claimed that the public knew exactly what he meant by causing "pain" in his marriage and that they appreciated Clinton being so forthcoming.

He stayed with the argument that he was being candid when Kroft asked if voters would wonder why Clinton would not deny adultery outright: "That may be what they're saying. You know what I think they're saying? I think they're saying, 'Here's a guy who's leveling with us'" (*60 Minutes,* January 26, 1992). Again, Clinton's discourse pointed to his supposed honesty in dealing with the public. He continued: "I have told the American people more than any other candidate for president" (*60 Minutes,* January 26, 1992). It is quite clear that Clinton's argument here was that he disclosed more than other candidates. In this way, he bolstered his character.

Finally, Clinton answered Kroft's query as to whether he had "leveled" with the public: "I have absolutely leveled with the American people" (*60 Minutes,* January 26, 1992). Again, he argued that he had done the moral and appropriate thing.

Attack Accuser

At various times in the interview, Clinton also chose to attack his accusers as a way of taking attention away from his alleged wrongdoing. For instance, he took the press to task for its handling of the issue: "And I think what the press has to decide is—are we going to engage in a game of gotcha" (*60 Minutes,* January 26, 1992). This statement attacks the media for pressing for details and making a game of the situation. Recall that he did not admit explicitly that he had an affair. His stated reason for this was because he predicted that the admission would not lay the issue to rest, that the press would then move on to the details of who the women were and dredging up more sordid information. In fact, he lamented the press's reaction to his presumed honesty in dealing with the issue (the honesty he used to bolster): "The result of that has been everybody going to my state and spending more time trying to play gotcha" (*60 Minutes,* January 26, 1992). Here again, Clinton attacked the press's handling of the issue.

He summarized his attitude about the media's tactics:

> You know, you can cut this round or you can cut this flat. I mean, if you deny, then you have a whole other hoard of people going down there offering more money trying to prove that you lied. And if you say yes, you have just what I've already said by being open and telling you that we've had problems. You have, oh, good, now we can play gotcha and find out who it is. Now no matter what I say to pretend that the press will then let this die, we're kidding ourselves. (*60 Minutes,* January 26, 1992)

Clearly, Clinton attacked the press again as being uninterested in anything other than a tabloid treatment of his alleged infidelity.

Finally, Clinton turned the character issue on the news media when Kroft asked him if his interview (now completed) succeeded in putting the issue behind him: "That's up to the American people, and to some extent, up to the press. This will test the character of the press. It is not only my character that has been tested" (*60 Minutes,* January 26, 1992). In short, the attack in this statement implies that the press misbehaved, at least to the extent that its collective character should be questioned.

Interestingly, Clinton's attacks concentrated largely on the media's role in the proliferation of allegations. Gennifer Flowers, who gave the media the information (or misinformation according to Clinton), remained relatively unscathed. However, Clinton did question her veracity: "It was only when money came out, wh—when the tabloid went down there offering people money to say that they had been involved with me that she changed her story" (*60 Minutes,* January 26, 1992). This undoubtedly functioned to attack Flowers' credibility by implying her story was financially motivated. As mentioned earlier, he also used Flowers' alleged statements in his denials, which implied that she was lying.

Clinton also managed to make a preemptive attack on any future accusers: "There is a recession on. Times are tough, and—and I think you can expect more and more of these stories as long as they're down there handing out money" (*60 Minutes,* January 26, 1992). In other words, Clinton said that the credibility of those who would accuse him of adultery was worthless since the stories would be fabrications composed in order to help themselves financially.

In summary, one should note that Clinton did attack his accusers. Moreover, the attacks pertained partially to their journalistic character and partially to their economic opportunism.

Transcendence

Clinton also attempted to defend himself by placing the alleged wrongdoing in a much larger, more important context. For example, consider what Clinton said when Kroft asked if he would deny ever having an extramarital affair: "I'm not prepared tonight to say that any married couple should ever discuss that with anyone but themselves. I'm not prepared to say that about anybody" (*60 Minutes,* January 26, 1992). Here, he made the point that the relationship between married people is sacrosanct and ought to be off limits to public discussion. It was implied that the integrity of the relationship had more importance than the press's demand for information. Kroft noted that Clinton had been making that same argument for a couple of months, to which the governor replied, "But that's what I believe" (*60 Minutes,* January 26. 1992). That interjection certainly augments his argument that the marital privacy at issue is more important than the scandal, and that he believed this sincerely.

Clinton later advanced his argument more specifically:

You know, I can remember a time—and it was sad—when a divorced person couldn't run for president. And that time, thank goodness, has passed. Nobody's prejudiced against anybody because they're divorced. Are we going to take the reverse position now—that if people have problems in their marriage or things in their past which they don't want to discuss, which are painful to them, that they can't run? (*60 Minutes,* January 26, 1992)

Again, Clinton made the point that the allegations were not germane to performing presidential duties. Moreover, he argued that society had passed the time when personal indiscretions or shortcomings disqualified candidates.

He reiterated the marital privacy issue:

There isn't a person watching this who would feel comfortable sitting on this couch detailing everything that ever went on in their life or their marriage. And I think it's real dangerous in this country if we don't have some zone of privacy for everybody. I mean, that is absolutely critical. (*60 Minutes,* January 26, 1992)

This passage continued the argument that at least some of the details of a candidate's (and presumably, his) personal life should not be subject to public scrutiny.

Clinton used transcendence again, placing the allegations in the context of the then economic woes of New Hampshire and the country:

And let's go on and get back to the real problems of this country. The problems are about what's going to happen to families in New Hampshire and the rest of this country in the future, not what happened to mine in the past. (*60 Minutes,* January 26, 1992)

This passage provided the argument that his alleged marriage problems were not really problems at all. The real problems were economic.

Finally, Clinton transcended again when Kroft pointed to a CBS survey that showed 14 percent of the electorate could not vote for someone guilty of adultery:

I know it's an issue. And—and—but what does that mean? That means 86% of the American people either don't think it's relevant to presidential performance or look at whether a person looking at all the facts is the best person to serve. (*60 Minutes,* January 26, 1992)

In short, his last transcendent argument asserted that electing a president should be about considering all of the facts and issues, not focusing on an irrelevant issue of fidelity. Marital privacy, national issues, and leadership capabilities were all more important than the matter at hand.

Differentiation

There were only two brief instances of differentiation, but they were both pivotal to Clinton's persuasive self-defense. First, Clinton differentiated his relationship with Flowers as friendly, as distinct from romantic: "She was an acquaintance. I would say a friendly acquaintance" (*60 Minutes,* January 26, 1992). This statement served to clarify how Clinton would represent the relationship—friendly, but not romantic. Upon first glance, the statement may appear to be a denial. However, I would argue that the substance of the statement sought to describe the way in which the relationship was different from a marital betrayal. Yes, he had a relationship with Flowers, but she was a friendly acquaintance, as distinct from a romantic interest.

Second, Clinton took issue with Kroft's intimation that his marriage to Hillary was strictly an arrangement of convenience: "Wait a minute. You're looking at two people who love each other. This is not an arrangement or an understanding. This is a marriage. That's a very different thing" (*60 Minutes,* January 26, 1992). Again, this might appear more like denial. However, Clinton's own language, "That's a very different thing," hinted at differentiation. He admitted that the marriage had not been perfectly blissful, but it remained intact and loving. He wanted his audience to understand that situation as distinct from a marriage of convenience. In short, Clinton wanted it clarified that his marriage was sincere, not merely expedient.

The above examples demonstrate how Clinton used denial, bolstering, attack accuser, transcendence, and differentiation to repair his image. The next section will take up assessment of the discourse.

EVALUATION

The evaluation of Clinton's discourse concerning the Flowers allegations will begin with an examination of the internal consistency and plausibility of the various strategies. After that, external corroborating evidence will be offered to assess the effectiveness of Clinton's image restoration.

Internal Consistency and Plausibility

Clinton's use of denial was not only fitting, but arguably, necessary, in order for him to continue as a viable candidate. Clearly, he nuanced his answers to Kroft's various questions throughout the interview. For instance, rather than offering a direct denial of an affair he said: "I've said that before and so has she." Here, he merely confirmed that both he and Flowers had made a denial in the past. When questioned, he made no current denial. He chose instead to say only that he had denied the allegations previously. This did not pose a current denial of the allegation at hand. Also, his denial of a twelve–year affair may have been evasive: "That allegation is false." That statement may have denied only that the affair was twelve years long, not that an affair took place. One could say that he offered very carefully worded responses where a simple "yes" or "no" would suffice as an answer.

One might question whether this skepticism toward Clinton's discourse is "nit-picking" and posing petty objections. Unfortunately, it is wholly reasonable to believe that he may have been twisting the language in such ways. Other chapters in this study will detail now infamous examples of Clinton's abuse of the language in order to deny wrongdoing (e.g., his assertion that he did not have sexual relations with Monica Lewinsky is the most notable).

Clinton's use of bolstering in the interview was also called for. When he pointed to his unprecedented disclosure of personal information, he implicitly argued that he was more honest, not less. His self-proclaimed forthcoming nature served to demonstrate a willingness to clarify, rather than conceal, his personal problems. Given that his overall character was in question during this period, it was probably a wise decision to illustrate his good character. The question of whether he was forthcoming by choice is irrelevant. His ability to bolster his character was the most relevant issue.

The way that Clinton went about attacking his accuser was well-advised. With feminists as a considerable Democratic voting base, it was wise to avoid a more direct attack on Flowers. Moreover, it served the dual purpose of condemning the source of the allegations (Flowers) and the mode of distribution (the media). Specifically, Flowers was discredited for allegedly changing her story when the tabloid was offering money. Simultaneously, the media were discredited for running and repeating the gossipy details. Both of these facts may have mitigated the potential for damage to Clinton's character.

Transcendence was an apt strategy, especially considering the political climate of the time. The American economy was in recession at the time and New Hampshire, like much of New England, was in particularly bad shape. Since there was so much anxiety about the state of the economy, Clinton's insistence that the media focus on "the issues" was likely to be well received. In this sense, Clinton's transcendence met the three criteria set by Benoit and Wells (1998). The economic pain of the region was assuredly more important to Democratic primary voters than Clinton's immorality. Clinton's appearance on *60 Minutes* testified to the distraction posed by the charges. Finally, Clinton's strong showing in New Hampshire (as illustrated by the external data) showed that the audience perceived that Clinton was capable of addressing the issues that were taking a backseat to the scandal.

Finally, Clinton's differentiation was necessary during this interview. When Kroft referred to Bill and Hillary's marriage as an "arrangement," Clinton had to describe the unique situation as something other than a marriage of convenience. In a time when the dissolution of the family could be blamed for numerous societal pathologies, Clinton needed to be perceived as committed to his family.

Clinton's chosen strategies were appropriate. External corroboration supported this evaluation.

Polling Data

An ABC News (1992) poll asked a national sample of adults whether they approved or disapproved of Clinton's explanation during his appearance on *60 Minutes*. The results showed that fully 70 percent approved of his remarks, 22 percent disapproved, and 8 percent did not know or had no opinion. Given that the specific subject at hand was the *60 Minutes* explanation, these numbers bode well for his image repair efforts.

Another ABC News poll (1992) had even better news for Clinton. The day after the interview, a combined 76 percent of respondents said that the allegations of adultery would either make no difference in their votes or make them slightly *more* likely to vote for him. Ten percent said they were somewhat less likely to vote for him, while only 10 percent said they were much less likely to vote for him because of the infidelity charge.

Interestingly, Clinton's attack on the news media's character may have been well received by the public. A *Times-Mirror* (1992) poll showed that only 8 percent of the public thought that newspapers and news programs had covered the charges "very responsibly." Another 36 percent said they covered the story "fairly responsibly." Twenty-four percent thought they acted "not too responsibly," and another 17 percent rated the coverage as "not at all responsibly." This information was rather damning for the news media. The news media require, at minimum, public confidence that they will conduct themselves fairly and responsibly. Otherwise, news products, their stock in trade, would be jeopardized. This data demonstrates a moderate-to-poor rating of public confidence. Some of this could be attributed to Clinton's charge that the media were more interested in playing "gotcha" than covering the vital issues of the campaign.

Commentary

Editorials and letters to the editor from the *New York Times* indicate that Clinton's image repair was successful. Columnist Leslie Gelb (1992) opined:

> Bill and Hillary Clinton decided they had to expose themselves to such a trial last night. On the distinguished CBS News program "60 Minutes," they repeated that their marriage had been troubled and re-affirmed that they have worked things out. That tells us everything we need to know. More than we need to know. (p. A21)

Gelb agreed with Clinton's claim that he had provided adequate information. Moreover, she also adopted his prediction of how the press would have reacted had he offered more information: "Bill Clinton does not pretend to sainthood. And it serves no public good or reason to further molest him about his private life and try to make him into a liar. And then hang him for that" (p. A21). In this statement, Gelb not only agrees with Clinton's decision to stop short of more details, but adds an attack on the media accusers, calling them molesters, in effect.

A *New York Times* editorial glowed with praise of Clinton's handling of the issue:

> At times, voters can legitimately ask about a political candidate's financial, sexual, or other personal conduct; it can bear on one's capacity for public service. At other times, any such inquiry amounts to no more than leers, smears, or smug moralizing. So far at least, Gov. Bill Clinton of Arkansas and his wife have found a reasonable place to draw a line between the two . . . they make a plausible case; there can be some preserve of privacy, even for politicians. . . . For lack of satisfactory evidence, most journalists declined to publish stories about Mr. Clinton's personal life. . . . Because the tape recordings she [Flowers] so far proffers don't appear to refute that characterization, there seems to be little basis for demanding further comment from the Clintons. (Eisenberg, January 28, 1992, p. A20)

In summary, some of Clinton's arguments were paraphrased in this editorial, suggesting the writer found them persuasive. For instance, the editorial agreed with Clinton's statement that marital privacy was imperative. Moreover, it implicitly accepted Clinton's denial of an affair with Flowers when the paper pointed to a lack of conclusive evidence that the affair took place.

Columnist A. M. Rosenthal (1992) was even more glowing, calling the Clinton's *60 Minutes* appearance a "gift" to the American people: "The gift is that they treated us as adults. The opportunity is for us to act that way" (p. A21). In other words, the allegations themselves presented the unique opportunity to adopt, in Rosenthal's opinion, a more grown-up attitude. For this, presumably, we had the Clintons to thank. The praise kept coming:

> They said there was no 12–year affair—and that the rest, if there is any, is their own business to deal with. Vote for the Governor if that position satisfies you, said the Clinton couple, do not if you think more should be squeezed out of us. I think that for now many American voters will accept that position of the Clintons. (p. A21)

This passage indicated that Clinton's denial and transcendence were taken to heart. Moreover, it assessed the image repair as well done and likely to be well received by the public.

Rosenthal (1992) also echoed Clinton's predictions that the Flowers incident could be followed by other unsubstantiated accusations: "Any new charge against Mr. Clinton will find a buyer . . . if so, what then? Will we condemn the Governor without a trial?" (p. A21). In short, attacks of this nature were to be expected now, and the credibility of their sources needed to be scrutinized.

Ted Van Dyk (1992) approved of Clinton's discourse:

> With style and shrewdness, Gov. Bill Clinton appears to have beaten the rap on his philandering and emerged stronger than he was before the Gennifer Flowers episode came up. Unless a second shoe (or bedroom slipper) drops to indicate he's a liar, his national exposure during his troubles has helped establish him more clearly as the Democrats' front-runner and likely nominee. (p. A20)

Here, the prognosis for successful image repair was also quite favorable. The article predicted not only recovery from the scandal, but domination of the Democratic field of candidates as part of the spoils.

A letter to the editor from Daniel Eisenberg (1992) of New York weighed in favorably as well:

> The surge in interest in the personal life of Gov. Bill Clinton of Arkansas, who is campaigning for the Democratic Party's Presidential nom-

ination, shows a disturbing trend in American politics . . . there is little
evidence in history to support the view that with moral piety comes
political effectiveness. (p. A21)

While this letter did not attest directly to Clinton's image repair efforts, it
did hint at the notion that presidential leadership qualifications transcended
personal transgressions. In this sense, it was consistent with Clinton's pro-
scription that the issues be the topic of interest.

Only one commentator remained skeptical of Clinton in the wake of the
scandal. Columnist Russell Baker (1992) wrote a television show parody
called "Meet the Adulterer," wherein he poked fun at Clinton's situation
and implied that his explanations were bizarre and insincere.

The polling data indicated that Clinton's discourse was well received.
Commentary was largely approving as well.

CONCLUSION

In the face of allegations that he committed adultery and maintained a
twelve–year love affair with Gennifer Flowers, Clinton used five strategies:
denial, bolstering, attack accuser, transcendence, and differentiation. They
were universally appropriate for the given charges and situation. He only
made one categorical denial of the affair, but employed more implicit denials throughout the interview as well. Also notable was his dual attack on accusers directed at Flowers, the source of the allegations, and the news
media, the distributor of the sordid details.

Commentary and letters in the *New York Times* largely approved of
Clinton's discourse and candidacy. Perhaps even more importantly, public
opinion polling showed a positive demeanor toward Clinton and a simulta-
neous negativity toward the press after the now infamous *60 Minutes* interview.

Chapter Five

"But I Didn't Inhale": The Marijuana Controversy

In this chapter, Clinton's limited discourse explaining his use of marijuana as an Oxford University student will be analyzed to discover which image restoration strategies he used and to what public reaction.

THE PERSUASIVE ATTACK

During a March 29, 1992, Democratic primary debate in New York, presidential candidate Bill Clinton admitted to smoking marijuana. Since marijuana is illegal in the United States, this admission clearly had the potential to hurt his candidacy. Moreover, in response to earlier press questions about drug use, he had replied, "I have never broken the laws of my country" (Edsall, 1992b). His admission of drug use while in England did not technically contradict his assertion of never disobeying American law. However, the carefully worded answer risked sounding evasive, something which a candidate for the presidency would want to avoid.

Columnist George Will (1992) took issue with Clinton's choice of words: "Is he again slaloming like a downhill skier, past semantic flags he carefully positioned, as he did about marital problems and the draft?" (p. A27). Balz and Broder (1992) documented how party insiders quietly began considering Representative Dick Gephardt and New York Governor Mario Cuomo as possible late entrants into the primaries.

Clinton needed to repair his image quickly. He needed to address three accusations: (1) that he had used marijuana, an illegal drug (though one should properly understand that Clinton admitted this prior to this accusation), (2) that he had been evasive in his earlier statements about marijuana use, and (3) that the revelation would hurt him politically.

THE PERSUASIVE DEFENSE

In this section, the strategies Clinton used to repair his image following his admission of marijuana use will be considered. The discourse examined is the brief series of statements made by Clinton which appeared in a CNN report on March 29, 1992. Clinton used the minimization and denial strategies. They will be discussed in that order.

Minimization

Clinton's use of minimization was found in his now infamous remark: "When I was in England, I experimented with marijuana a time or two and I didn't like it, and I didn't inhale and never tried it again" (Clinton admits, 1992). In this statement, Clinton admitted to using marijuana, but minimized the extent to which he used it. By saying that he did not inhale the substance, he implied that the action was not as bad as if he had actually imbibed the substance.

When he claimed to have "experimented . . . a time or two," he minimized the offense as well. These words implied that the use was isolated and done merely out of curiosity, not an adopted lifestyle practice.

By saying that he did not like the experience and never repeated it, he minimized the offense, implying that he never became an active part of the drug culture that so many people found offensive. This example shows how Clinton used minimization to repair his image.

Denial

Clinton used denial for two purposes. First, he denied that his admission would harm his chances for election. Second, he denied having mislead anybody about his drug use.

When asked if his admission created any political damage to his candidacy, he was mindful of admissions by other past candidates: "Well, I don't think it hurt Senator [Albert of Tennessee] Gore four years ago, or Governor [Bruce of Arizona] Babbitt. It certainly didn't keep Clarence Thomas off the Supreme Court. So I don't know" (Clinton admits, 1992). Even though he said, "I don't know," his listing of those notable people who had not suffered from their admissions of marijuana use implied that he was denying that his admission would harm him politically.

Clinton's second denial dealt with assertions of what he said to inquiring parties. Recall that he had told the *New York Daily News* that he had never broken the laws of the United States. He bristled at the question of why he had not admitted the pot smoking to that editorial board:

> They said, "You never answered this," and I said, "Yeah, I've answered," and they said, "What did you answer before?" and I told them what I had answered before. I was on the way out of the *Daily News* interview. If they had asked me the same question that she [the questioner at the New York debate] did, I would give them the same answer. (Clinton admits, 1992)

Here, Clinton denied lying about his drug use to previous questioners. Both of these examples show how Clinton used denial to repair his image.

EVALUATION

Clinton's marijuana-related discourse can be judged by two criteria. First, it will be judged for internal consistency and plausibility. Second, external reaction in *New York Times* commentary and public opinion polling data will be considered.

Internal Consistency and Plausibility

Clinton's use of minimization was probably appropriate insofar as it underscored the point that Clinton claimed he was not an active part of the 1960s drug scene. Had Clinton engaged in frequent, repeated drug use the public might have had more reason to question his judgment. It was probably also helpful that Clinton claimed he had not enjoyed the experience. Had Clinton communicated that he enjoyed the illegal activity, the public may have perceived him as disrespectful of law and order.

However, Clinton's assertion that he did not inhale the smoke was fodder for comedians for weeks. To this day, people ridicule the statement and laugh at its silliness. Presumably, Clinton had hoped to minimize his participation in the illegal act by claiming that the intoxicating element, for example, the smoke, was never consumed. He should have simply stated the infrequency of the drug abuse and his disdain for the experience.

His denial that the admission would hurt his electoral chances by making him appear morally deficient was probably appropriate. Both Senator Gore and Governor Babbitt had admitted marijuana use. Neither won the nomination in 1988, but there is no evidence that their admissions played any part in their falling short. Moreover, Supreme Court Justice Clarence Thomas admitted to isolated drug use while in college and went on to be confirmed as a member of the high court. Quite arguably, experimentation with marijuana during the 1960s and 1970s may have been so rampant that the public is not outraged that some partook of marijuana in their youth. Of course, Supreme Court nominee Douglas Ginsburg admitted to marijuana use and ultimately withdrew his nomination in 1987. However, Ginsburg had admitted to smoking pot just seven years earlier (Edsall, 1992a), which may have been perceived more as indicative of weak character than a youthful indiscretion.

Finally, Clinton's denial that he had not lied before when asked about his drug use may have been technically accurate. However, his ultimate admission of having smoked marijuana showed how he had been evasive earlier. Evasiveness could surely hurt one's credibility as a candidate. As such, that strategy was ill-advised. To Clinton's benefit, the electorate didn't consider trying marijuana to be a very serious offense. In other words, his defense was not very powerful, but the accusations were not that damaging.

Polling Data

Public opinion polling indicates that Clinton's discourse was not wholly successful. When asked about Clinton's handling of the marijuana issue, 65 percent said it had "not much effect," while 24 percent had a "less favorable" view of Clinton and 9 percent had a "more favorable" view (Public Opinion Online, 1992). In short, his handling may have hurt him more than it helped him, but it had no huge effect. Interestingly, 68 percent of those polled believed Clinton's assertion that he never inhaled the marijuana was a lie (Public Opinion Online, 1992).

Commentary

A *New York Times* editorial, while not mentioning the marijuana explicitly, complained that the news media should not engage in a game of "get the candidates." Forgiveness of Clinton's misdeed was implicit (Get the candidates, 1992, p. A20).

Columnist Anna Quindlen predicted that Clinton's marijuana use would not ultimately hurt his candidacy. However, she offered him the advice that he should have simply admitted to smoking marijuana without explaining further:

Never explain. One result was that Billy Crystal, who has made the Oscar telecast finally worth staying awake for, looked into the camera the other night and said, "Didn't inhale?" to a great guffaw from the audience. Mr. Clinton's suggestion that he smoked dope without inhaling made him look like either a fibber or a dork. (Quindlen, 1992b, p. A25)

In short, Quindlen approved of his denial, but ridiculed his assertion that he had not inhaled.

A. M. Rosenthal opined that the public should not let the marijuana admission (and the ensuing media circus) distract people from listening to Clinton: "The question is no longer whether Bill Clinton will prove himself smart enough for New York Democrats. It is whether they will show themselves smart enough, mature and sophisticated enough to listen to the man" (Rosenthal, 1992, p. A29).

In short, Rosenthal did not even consider the marijuana issue when assessing Clinton as a candidate. Moreover, the *New York Times* ultimately gave its strongest stamp of approval when it endorsed Clinton in the New York Democratic primary (For George Bush, 1992).

All of the above commentaries provide evidence that Clinton's image remained at least preferable to the other Democratic candidates. Additionally, the relatively low amount of commentary on the issue in the papers (and none of it negative) may serve as a barometric reading that the public was not outraged over the admission of pot smoking.

CONCLUSION

Clearly, Clinton's winning of the Democratic nomination combined with a lack of outrage in the letters-to-the-editor section bespeaks of a public that did not take too much offense to his statements. However, according to polling, more people reacted negatively than positively to his handling of the issue. Moreover, the public thought his "didn't inhale" statement was a lie. People still laugh at the silliness of that defense.

In summary, Clinton's handling of the issue, though ridiculous at one point, was not met with outrage. This underscores the seriousness of a given charge in image restoration. However, a simple admission of having smoked pot might have been more effective than his convoluted and laughable statements. His discourse should be evaluated as mediocre, knowing that a more forthcoming answer could have made a less-than-damning accusation even less a distraction to his campaign.

Chapter Six

Land Ho!: Whitewater

Between January 3, 1994, and August 3, 1994, President Bill Clinton addressed the "Whitewater" matter in the course of seven press/media appearances. This chapter will first explain the allegations against Clinton and then analyze his discourse in these settings using Benoit's (1995a) typology of image restoration strategies. Note that this chapter, which considers discourse from multiple dates, will examine texts chronologically within the strategy categories. Finally, the discourse will be evaluated, considering internal merit and external data as evidence of effectiveness.

THE PERSUASIVE ATTACK

The scandal commonly referred to as "Whitewater" is a complicated matter. In its largest incarnation, it encompasses alleged financial, ethical, governmental, and sexual misdeeds. For a detailed description of the investigation, the reader should see the *Washington Post Online* (1998) special report devoted to the matter.

A brief history of this subject reveals, essentially, a bad real estate investment coupled with corruption, possibly on the part of the Clintons. In 1978, Governor and Mrs. Clinton, along with James and Susan McDougal, bought 220 acres of land in Arkansas, forming the Whitewater Development Corporation. The development project was a failure and dissolved in 1992, leaving the Clintons a $40,000 loss. Jim McDougal also owned Madison Guaranty Savings and Loan, which went under (costing taxpayers) in the 1980s. Hillary Clinton acted as legal counsel for the S&L. Both McDougals were convicted of fraud related to the failed development. Arkansas Governor Jim Guy Tucker was also convicted (*Washington Post Online,* 1998).

Much of the controversy in Whitewater centered around a fraudulent $300,000 loan to Susan McDougal, some portion of which was funneled to the Whitewater Development Corporation. Former Little Rock judge David Hale, whose company issued the loan, testified that then-Governor Clinton pressured Hale to make the loan.

Also central was the disappearance and reappearance of billing records indicating Hillary Clinton had done legal work for Madison. The records had been subpoenaed two years prior and were ultimately found in the White House private quarters.

Republican U.S. Representative James A. Leach (1993) described the allegations in a *Washington Post* op-ed piece:

> What some describe as "Whitewater-gate" is all about the role of then-Gov. Clinton in allowing a state-chartered savings and loan, declared insolvent by federal regulators, to continue not only to accept insured deposits but to grow exponentially for half a decade in the 1980s as a private piggy bank for insiders and the Arkansas political establishment. What also is at issue is the former governor's partnership with James McDougal, the S&L's president, in a murky real estate development called Whitewater. The facts are incomplete but simple. An S&L that received favored inattention by state regulators cost the federal taxpayers approximately $50 million when its doors closed, a sum that represented almost one-half of the institution's deposit base. (p. A21)

Clinton needed to address four accusations: (1) that he wielded illegal influence over a lending institution in his state in order to secure real estate loans, (2) that he and his wife hindered investigators by withholding requested materials, (3) that he improperly contacted a controlling legal authority in the investigation (the Resolution Trust Corporation) and (4) that his wife's legal work on behalf of Madison Guaranty Savings and Loan, the S&L in question, presented a conflict of interest.

One should note that the Whitewater matter is quite complicated. I have attempted to describe the context of Clinton's defensive discourse throughout the analysis section.

THE PERSUASIVE DEFENSE

Over the eight-month period examined in this chapter, Clinton relied on bolstering, simple denial, and transcendence in his image repair discourse. He also engaged in defeasibility, differentiation, minimization, attack accuser, shift blame, corrective action, and mortification. The strategies will be discussed in that order, beginning with Clinton's most prevalent strategies and proceeding to those strategies he employed less often.

Bolstering

Clinton's discourse in the Whitewater matter was replete with bolstering. The vast majority of the bolstering dealt with his self-proclaimed forthcoming nature. For instance, in his remarks at a health care press briefing, he commented, "I've said we would turn the records over. There is nothing else for me to say about that" (Clinton, 1994a, p. 3). Although rather short, that statement served to underscore his compliance with investigators' requests.

In a lengthy press conference, he bolstered several times more. For instance, he reiterated his willingness to cooperate:

The investigation of Whitewater is being handled by an independent special counsel whose appointment I supported. Our cooperation with counsel has been total. We have supplied over 14,000 documents, my tax returns dating back to 1978, and made available every administration witness he has sought. (Clinton, 1994b, p. 3)

Here, Clinton enhanced his image by indicating that he favored the appointment of the special counsel and had cooperated fully. Presumably, only honest people would be so willing to accommodate scrutiny.

The subject of bolstering turned to his attitude toward the investigation:

I think what's important is that I answer the questions that you have that are legitimate questions; that I fully cooperate with the special counsel, which was requested widely by the press and by the members of the Republican Party, and who is himself a Republican—that we fully cooperate. And we've done that. (Clinton, 1994b, p. 8)

In this statement Clinton argued that his set of priorities included a full investigation into the charges and that he had been helpful. As further evidence that he had cooperated, he borrowed the testimony of a Democratic senator: "Senator Inouye from Hawaii pointed out today, he said, I've been experienced in these investigations. He said, you folks have claimed no executive privilege. You've cooperated fully. No one can quarrel with that" (Clinton, 1994b, p. 8). Clearly, this statement served to reaffirm Clinton's perception as a forthcoming, willing participant.

Next, his bolstering turned to a description of his general motivation for public service:

> I'm like most of you—I gave my records every year to an accountant; and I told them to resolve it out in favor of the government. I never wanted anybody questioning whether I had paid the taxes that I owed, because I wasn't in my line of work for the money. (Clinton, 1994d, p. 14)

This explanation reinforced the argument that Clinton had cooperated beyond expectations, and went further in asserting that he was not driven by financial gain, only public service. Such selflessness would surely be admirable to the public.

Clinton closed this press event with a reference to his long-standing reputation: "Let me just say this—I was elected governor of my state five times. No one ever—even my roughest enemies, my strongest opponents—never suggested that there was a hint of scandal in my administration" (Clinton, 1994d, p. 12).

The above examples of bolstering amply demonstrate Clinton's reliance on that strategy. Clinton praised himself for cooperating in the investigation, for favoring the appointment of the independent counsel, for his motivations for serving in public office, and for his general integrity.

Simple Denial

Clinton also used the simple denial strategy on several occasions. For instance, asked whether he owed any back taxes related to his Whitewater ownership, he flatly stated, "I do not believe we owe any back taxes" (Clinton, 1994b, p. 3). He also denied directly knowing of any federally insured money going into the Whitewater venture: "No. I have no knowledge of that. I have absolutely no knowledge of that" (Clinton, 1994b, p. 4).

Other times, his denials involved incorporating complex information in order to support denials. Referring to the issue of whether Clinton had lost as much money on the investment as he had reported, he appealed to forthcoming information:

> Tomorrow, my counsel, David Kendall, will brief the press on the evidence that we have, what's in the tax returns. You will see when you

see the tax returns that those losses were clearly there. And he will be glad to support it with other information as well. (Clinton, 1994b, p. 4)

In other words, Clinton sometimes offered evidence which would corroborate his denial, rather than just flatly denying wrongdoing.

Another strong denial was offered when asked if he had any knowledge of federal regulators trying to stop the Resolution Trust Corporation officers from referring the Whitewater matter for criminal investigation: "Absolutely not" (Clinton, 1994b). Here, the denial was unequivocal. He continued: "I can tell you categorically I had no knowledge of this and was not involved in it in any way" (Clinton, 1994b, p. 5). Moreover, on this issue of the Resolution Trust Corporation, Clinton wanted to be perfectly clear:

Let me just say again, I have had absolutely nothing to do, and would have nothing to do, with any attempt to influence an RTC regulatory matter. And I think if you look at the actions of the RTC just since I've been President and you examine the facts that everybody that works there was appointed by a previous Republican administration, the evidence is clear that I have not done that. (Clinton, 1994b, p. 5)

He made the same assertion at other times in the press conference as well. For instance, he assured the press, "I have had no contact with the RTC. I've made no attempt to influence them" (Clinton, 1994b, p. 10). Here again, the denial was direct and to the point. In each of these statements, blanket denials of knowledge of a cover-up were made.

Another denial dealt with the nature of the investment to begin with. Asked whether he made any mistakes in the initial investment or the White House's handling of the matter, Clinton asserted:

I certainly don't think I made a mistake in the initial investment. It was a perfectly honorable thing to do, and it was a perfectly legal thing to do. And I didn't make any money, I lost money. I paid my debts. And then later on, as you know, Hillary and I tried to make sure that the corporation was closed down in an appropriate way and paid any obligations that it owed after we were asked to get involved at a very late stage, and after Mr. McDougal had left the S&L. So, I don't think that we did anything wrong in that at all. And I think we handled it in an appropriate way. (Clinton, 1994b, p. 5)

Again, Clinton offered denials (both of making a questionable investment and then mishandling the fallout, accompanied by relevant information in support of a denial.

Addressing the question of whether the Clintons wielded an improper conflict of interest via Hillary's legal association with Madison Savings and Loan, Clinton continued his denials:

> Now, all I can do is tell you that she believed there was nothing unethical about it. And today, in an interview, Professor Steven Geller, of New York University, who is a widely respected national expert on legal ethics, once again said there was nothing at all unethical in doing this. (Clinton, 1994b, p. 9)

This statement served as a two-fold denial: nothing unethical occurred, and even if it did, Hillary believed there was nothing unethical in her work for Madison. If she was not aware of any ethical violation, she could not be morally accountable for any violation.

Clinton also engaged in denial when pressed for reasons why, when refusing to turn over documents earlier, he had acted as though he had something to hide: "I don't think I acted as if I had anything to hide" (Clinton, 1994b, p. 9). In other words, he denied acting as though he had done something wrong.

The preceding examples demonstrate the great extent to which Clinton used denial in his defensive discourse. Clinton denied: making tax filing improprieties; exerting influence over regulatory matters at the Resolution Trust Corporation; mishandling the Whitewater corporation investment and dissolution; possessing a conflict of interest through Hillary Clinton's work for Madison Guaranty Savings and Loan; and having anything to hide in general.

Transcendence

Clinton also used the transcendence strategy on numerous occasions. For instance, Clinton placed the allegations against him in context: "This is the best moment we've had in decades to do the hard work on so many issues that affect not only our own progress and prosperity, but the very way we think about ourselves as a nation" (Clinton, 1994b, p. 3). Here, the context of these remarks within Clinton's persuasive defense indicate that Clinton wanted the audience to focus on "bigger" issues.

Clinton used that strategy again to address the question of what he ought to be doing instead of attending to the allegations: "And then I get back to the work of getting unemployment down, jobs up, passing a health care bill, passing the crime bill, moving this country forward" (Clinton, 1994b, p. 8). In other words, Clinton argued that the Whitewater questions at hand were not particularly important, certainly not part of any effort to move the country in a positive direction.

He proceeded with a prediction that the matter would be unimportant in the annals of history:

> None of this, in the light of history, will be as remotely as important as the fact that by common consensus we had the most productive first year of a presidency last year of anyone in a generation. That's what matters; that we're changing people's lives. That's what counts. (Clinton, 1994b, p. 8)

In short, he insisted that the allegations were, ultimately, not important because they were not part of the productive efforts to impact people's lives. Perhaps in complement to his transcendence, Clinton added some bolstering over the first year of his presidency.

Clinton also used transcendence to place the temporal nature of the allegations in context: "Consider this, has any other previous president ever had to say, here's what we did 16, 17 years ago?" (Clinton, 1994d, p. 12). This statement pointed to the unimportance of the matter at hand compared to things the presidency usually dealt with. He continued with the temporal transcendence theme: "Let me be president in 1994, while somebody else worries about what happened in 1979. . . . I need to go about being President, worrying about the problems of the American people in 1994" (Clinton, 1994d, p. 12). Again, the allegations were portrayed as inconsequential to the country's business.

On another occasion, Clinton used transcendence to belittle the charges against him:

> The only thing I've ever asked of them [Congress] is not to let any of this stuff interfere with the business of the people. . . . We've got big work to do, and my only concern is let's just keep putting the business of this country first. (Clinton, 1994e, p. 3)

In short, Clinton argued, the issues of government were of the utmost priority and dwarfed the accusations in level of importance.

Each of the above examples demonstrate how Clinton attempted to make the substantial efforts of his presidency the primary focus of the public. Furthermore, each time the strategy was employed, the Whitewater allegations were placed in a larger context that could presumably make the charges less menacing. He described the charges as either unimportant or inconsequential to history.

Defeasibility

Clinton also used the defeasibility strategy several times for the purpose of placing certain matters beyond his control. For instance, asked by the press to explain discrepancies over how much money he had borrowed from Madison Guaranty Savings and Loan, he pointed to a financial transaction he claimed to have overlooked:

> And so I started racking my brain to try to remember what that might have been, and by coincidence, I was also rereading the galleys of my mother's autobiography, just fact checking it, and I noticed that she mentioned there something that I had genuinely forgotten, which is that I helped her to purchase the property and what was then a cabin on the place that she and her husband, Dick Kelley, lived back in 1981, and that I was a co-owner of that property with her for just a few months. After they married, he bought my interest out. (Clinton, 1994b, p. 3)

This passage serves to show that some information he could have been providing was simply forgotten. In short, he could not help withholding information because his memory faculty had failed him. He repeated the anecdote minutes later:

> So when he [James McDougal] said he didn't think this note that I—where I borrow money from a bank, not an S&L, in 1981 had anything to do with Whitewater, I started thinking about it. We talked about it. We couldn't remember what else it could have been until I literally just happened to cross that in reading my mother's autobiography. (Clinton, 1994b, p. 5)

Here again, the omission is attributed to the inability to retrieve the information in question. In brief remarks to the press pool the following day, Clinton reiterated this accounting of the events:

> And what happened was, when I read my mother's autobiography, I said, you know, that's right, I did help her buy that place. And then—so Hillary and I were talking, so we asked for the checks. And

when I saw the check, then I realized that that's where it had come from. (Clinton, 1994c, p. 2)

In short, he repeated the explanation of how his memory, which originally failed him, had been jarred.

One other instance of defeasibility demonstrated Clinton's argument that he did not have the information necessary to adequately inform him: "I always did what I think most Americans do, I gave all my records every year to my accountant" (Clinton, 1994c, p. 2). In other words, he did not even possess the information needed to recall pertinent information. Notably, this statement did not shift the blame to the accountant. It merely explained how reasonable it was that Clinton could not recall some important things. These examples illustrate the president's use of defeasibility in order to evade responsibility for alleged wrongdoing.

Differentiation

Clinton used differentiation on multiple occasions as well. For instance, a questioner asked Clinton about a recent comment by Representative Jim Leach. The reporter's question assumed that Leach's statement functioned to accuse Clinton of a cover-up. Clinton begged to differ:

Absolutely not. And it is my understanding that Mr. Leach was rather careful in the words that he used and apparently he didn't even charge that any political appointee of our administration had any knowledge of this. So he may be talking about an internal dispute within the RTC from career Republican appointees for all I know. (Clinton, 1994b, p. 5)

In short, he differentiated what Leach said from what the reporter implied in his/her question.

He used this strategy again in describing Hillary's legal activity:

I did not say—I said that when my wife did business, when her law firm represented some state agency itself—state agencies all over America use private lawyers—if she did any work for the state, she never took any pay for it. (Clinton, 1994b, p. 9)

Here, Clinton differentiated doing no work for the state and accepting money for work performed for the state. The distinction was important in order to avoid the charge of political corruption. Each of the above examples demonstrate Clinton's use of differentiation.

Minimization

Another strategy Clinton employed was minimization. For instance, Clinton argued that his co-ownership with his mother in the aforementioned land and cabin was fleeting: "I was a co-owner of that property with her for just a few months. After they married, he [Mrs. Kelley's husband] bought my interest out" (Clinton, 1994b, p. 3). This statement minimized the length of time that the partnership lasted.

Next, Clinton sought to minimize Hillary's role in the legal work done for Madison:

> Basically the firm wrote the securities commissioner a letter saying, is it permissible under Arkansas law to raise money for this S&L in this way? And it showed that she was one of the contacts on it, and the securities commissioner wrote her back and said it's not against the law. That was basically the extent of her representation. (Clinton, 1994b, p. 9)

In short, according to Clinton, Hillary's involvement with the Savings and Loan was limited to an inquiry to the securities commissioner. This surely served to minimize Hillary's involvement with the transactions related to Madison. The above examples show how Clinton used the minimization strategy in his image repair discourse.

Shift the Blame

The texts examined also exhibit blame shifting. For instance, his defense turned to the management of Whitewater: McDougal has "always told you that I had nothing to do with the management of Whitewater, that Hillary had nothing to do with it; we didn't keep the books or the records" (Clinton, 1994b, p. 4). This declaration implicitly shifts the blame to the person who did keep the books, McDougal. This example demonstrates Clinton's use of blame shifting in his image repair efforts.

Attack Accuser

Clinton attacked his accusers on two occasions. First, he attacked those who called for the investigation: "I mean, this decision which many called for is going to cost the taxpayers millions of dollars" (Clinton, 1994f, p. 3). This is an example of attacking those responsible for bringing accusations. In the other instance, he attacked the character of his accusers: "I have been the subject, sir, of false charges. People saying things about me that are not true don't make my credibility an issue. They make their credibility an issue, not mine" (Clinton, 1994d, p. 28). Here, Clinton said his attackers lacked credibility, which is surely an attack on their character. Notably, the attack also included a reference to his alleged victimization in the matter. This victimization may have served to further demonize his accusers for their inflictions. Both of these examples demonstrate Clinton's use of attacks on accusers. Of course, his assertion in this statement that the allegations are not true also served to deny.

Mortification

Clinton's Whitewater discourse contained instances of mortification as well. When asked about improper communication between his office and the Resolution Trust Corporation, he admitted, "I think that we weren't as sensitive as we should have been. And I've said before, it would have been better if that hadn't occurred" (Clinton, 1994b, p. 8). Although he did not explicitly express remorse over the misdeeds, he did admit that they should not have occurred. Notably, in the next sentence he went on to offer the transcendent argument that none of the matters at issue would amount to anything historically important. In short, the apology was short-lived.

Regarding the issue of why he delayed in turning over documents, Clinton offered a psuedo-apology: "Perhaps I should have done it earlier, but you will see essentially what I've told you—and things that you basically already know" (Clinton, 1994b, p. 10). In other words, he admitted wrongdoing (qualified by "perhaps"), but then qualified his apology. These examples show how Clinton used mortification in his image repair discourse.

Corrective Action

One instance of corrective action addressed the issue of back taxes that Clinton may have been delinquent on:

> When it turned out in our own investigation of this Whitewater business that one year we had inadvertently taken a tax deduction for interest payments when, in fact, it was principal payment, even though the statute of limitations had run out, we went back and voluntarily paid

what we owed to the federal government. And if it turns out we've
made some mistake inadvertently, we will do that again. (Clinton,
1994b, p. 6)

Here, Clinton said that when money was owed, it was paid up and offered a
promise of such behavior in the future. This is a clear example of corrective
action.

In review, Clinton used primarily bolstering, denial, and transcendence
in his Whitewater-related image repair efforts. However, he also used
defeasibility, differentiation, minimization, shifting blame, attack accuser,
mortification, and corrective action to a lesser extent.

EVALUATION

This discourse can be evaluated by two criteria. First, the image repair
strategies will be assessed in terms of internal consistency and plausibility.
Second, external data will be presented to gauge how well Clinton's discourse was received by the public.

Internal Consistency and Plausibility

Clinton's reliance on bolstering, denial, and transcendence made perfect
sense and embodied a powerful three-part defense. By bolstering his good
qualities in many relevant areas, Clinton advanced himself as uniquely
compliant and ethical throughout the investigation. For instance, he repeatedly claimed to be cooperating fully with investigators. If accepted as true,
this would certainly create the perception that he had nothing to hide. His
good qualities extended from areas of honesty and cooperativeness to disci-
plined focus on his responsibilities as president. These qualities are certainly valued by voters. For instance, he claimed not only that the matter
was no distraction, but that his first year in office was of historical merit.
This claim was plausible enough that it did not prompt follow-up questions
from the press.

His denials were also well-placed. He denied doing anything unethical or
illegal, which was important in this particular scenario. It is expected that
the president will be a law-abiding citizen with a clean ethical record as well
(although some might argue such importance is diminishing). As such, one
could argue that Clinton had to deny breaking the law or engaging in any financial irregularities.

To be sure, transcendence was appropriate as well. Clinton's transcendence argument posited that the issue at hand (a 1980s land deal and subse-

quent events) was not substantially relevant to the issues confronting the American people. Few could argue with this line of reasoning, though some could insist that morality is an issue in itself. In any case, this transcendence, combined with claims of innocence and virtue, could convince the public that (a) wrongdoing had not occurred, or (b) that the wrongdoing was not pertinent to their lives. There is no polling data showing that the public thought Clinton was distracted, but one could surmise from the amount of time he devoted to explaining Whitewater that it was a constant problem for him. Likewise, there is no data showing that the public thought Clinton could adequately address the issues being ignored at the time. However, he had won the presidency by a healthy margin two years before, indicating that at least a plurality of the public thought Clinton was competent enough to handle important issues. As such, Clinton again met the criteria for enhancing transcendence found in Benoit and Wells (1998).

The other strategies, though used less frequently, added to the image repair as well. For instance, by claiming that accountants handled his financial records, he made an excellent defeasibility argument. How could one be expected to recall detailed information, especially if someone else processed that data? Also notable in the other sundry strategies employed are the attacks on the accusers, who Clinton portrayed as playing cynical politics. Upon close scrutiny, there may appear to be some inconsistency here. Clinton said he had fully supported the investigation. Then he proceeded to attack the investigation as a waste of money. Still, his attack was consistent because being in favor of an investigation, in general, should not necessarily mean favoring the wasteful character of a particular investigation. Moreover, this attack remained plausible because of the sheer amounts of revenue spent for the inquiry.

In general, Clinton's choice of strategies proved appropriate in this matter. Of course, strategies like denying wrongdoing and bolstering one's cooperative nature might only be effective if they are not demonstrably false (such as Clinton's claim of cooperation). In this instance, however, Clinton's frequent and sustained claims to be cooperating with investigators could have plausibly convinced the audience that he had been compliant.

In an examination of Whitewater-related image repair of both Clintons, Benoit and Wells (1998) also evaluated Bill Clinton's defense as generally effective, though they had reservations about Hillary's discourse. Furthermore, one need only recognize Clinton's healthy political victory in the 1996 presidential election as further evidence that his handling of the issue was at least sufficient to ensure his short-term political survival.

Polling Data

The polling data reveals a mixed reception. A poll taken the week following Clinton's lengthy March 24, 1994, press conference found that 50
percent of the public approved of Clinton's handling of the Whitewater issue, with 40 percent disapproving. During this same period, however, a
combined 57 percent of those polled thought Clinton had done something
illegal (17 percent) or unethical (40 percent) (Public Opinion Online,
1994b).

By August, the public opinion dynamic had changed to some extent, but
still revealed mixed feelings from the public: a combined 38 percent of the
public thought Clinton had done something illegal (14 percent) or unethical
(24 percent). This reduction in the percentage of people who thought
Clinton had performed misdeeds could provide support for a positive evaluation of Clinton's image repair efforts, particularly the instances of denial.
However, a substantial 39 percent said they were unsure of whether misdeeds had taken place while only 22 percent said he did nothing wrong
(Public Opinion Online, 1994b). When only 22 percent of the population
believed the president's assertions of innocence, one might argue that he retained image problems.

Following the discourse period examined here, 61 percent of those
polled agreed with the *New York Times* that an independent counsel should
be appointed, lending support to the notion that the public may have thought
that Attorney General Reno's investigation was inadequate. This might
also mean that the president's bolstering of his compliance may not have
been accepted by the public.

Much to the president's benefit, however, a majority of the public
thought the Whitewater matter was either not important at all (25 percent)
or not too important (27 percent), while a minority thought the issue was
very important (17 percent) or somewhat important (26 percent) (Public
Opinion Online, 1994c). In other words, the president's transcendence
strategy may have resonated with the public. They agreed that the accusations were relatively unimportant.

Commentary

Commentaries and letters to the editor in the *New York Times* display a
mixed reaction. For instance, an editorial called for further scrutiny:

Legitimate suspicions have arisen that James McDougal—the
Clintons' land partner and operator of the defunct Madison Guaranty

Savings and Loan who helped the Clintons financially—may have benefited from lenient regulation when Mr. Clinton was Governor.... These long-simmering insinuations reached a boil two weeks ago with the news that White House aides removed files bearing on the real estate partnership from the office of Vincent Foster, the deputy White House counsel, after he committed suicide last spring. (Safire, 1994a, p. A14)

Such a call for further inquiry implies that, at least early on in the image repair campaign, the issue had not been put to rest.

Only days later, the *New York Times* editorialized again, blatantly accusing the Clintons of hindering the Whitewater investigation:

Is no one at the White House reading the history of recent Presidential scandals? These clumsy efforts at suppression are feckless and self-defeating. The White House's attempts to maintain political control of the investigation into President and Mrs. Clinton's real estate dealings in Arkansas are swiftly draining away public trust in their integrity.... Ms. Reno's department has called for documents including papers that the White House Counsel, Bernard Nussbaum, removed from the office of his deputy, Vincent Foster, after Mr. Foster's suicide last summer. (Safire, 1994b, p. A30)

This opinion disagrees sharply with Clinton's claim that he had been cooperative with investigators.

Columnist William Safire (1994a) took issue with Clinton's behavior in the investigation as well:

From the moment Foster's body was found, White House Counsel Bernard Nussbaum acted to keep those Whitewater files away from prying eyes. The investigation was confined to the Keystone-Kop Park Police; Clinton lawyers refused to let them or the FBI see papers that might have revealed the suicide motive; and then— secretly—the files were spirited away from the White House to the President's personal lawyer. (p. A21)

In short, Safire provided additional reasons for not believing Clinton's claim of compliance and forthrightness. Safire (1994b) wrote another commentary questioning Clinton's honesty:

The clank of falsity goes to the top. For over a year the White House has been saying that Whitewater files were sent from Vincent Foster's office after his death to the Clintons' private attorney. At a much-praised press conference in April, Hillary Clinton was asked if her top aide, Margaret Williams, had removed documents from Foster's office. "I don't think she did remove any documents," Mrs. Clinton answered. She said, "Mr. Nussbaum distributed the files according to whom he thought should have them." Sounds as if it went right to the family lawyer right? (p. A23)

Again, Safire provided a stinging indictment of the administration's ethics. Michael Wines (1994) lent support to Safire's moral assessment:

Rightly or wrongly, with each new element of the story—from disclosure to special prosecutor to new disclosure to hearings to independent counsel—the notion that the White House is somehow not playing by accepted rules becomes more embedded in the public's mind. (p. 26)

In short, Wines argued, public perception of Clinton was becoming compromised.

While much of the commentary surrounding Whitewater was unfavorable to the president, columnist Anthony Lewis (1994) provided some moral support for the Clintons:

One thing is indisputable about Whitewater. Despite some fumbling and evasion, the Clinton Administration has been forthcoming compared to the Bush and Reagan Administrations. It called for an independent counsel, and every official asked to testify has done so. (p. A25)

In other words, according to Lewis, Clinton had acted ethically compared to his two predecessors, "fumbling and evasion" not withstanding.

This sample of commentary reflects some of the meaning behind the polls indicating that Americans believed Clinton was hiding something, possibly something illegal/unethical. However, in contrast to the wider public, nothing in the columns indicated that these pundits believed the issue was unimportant.

CONCLUSION

Clinton's defensive discourse in the Whitewater matter had strengths and weaknesses. Denial was effective to the extent that his denials could not be demonstrated as false. His compliance-related bolstering was not particularly effective as evidenced by a public call for an independent counsel. However, one must conclude that Clinton's use of transcendence was effective given the public's agreement that the Whitewater matter was not particularly pressing.

Clinton's Whitewater-related discourse provided another example of the importance of the relative severity of accusations. The polling data showed that the public did not think Clinton was innocent in this matter. This indicates that his denials may not have been believable. His bolstering claims of cooperation are suspect for the same reason. However, the public clearly did not think the matter was serious. One could certainly argue that allegations of financial irregularities, and subsequent attempts to hide them, are serious matters. The fact that the public did not find the allegations against Clinton troubling (i.e., those described in this chapter), may speak volumes about Clinton's successful use of transcendence. Either the allegations were unimportant, or Clinton successfully persuaded Americans of their relative lack of salience. I would argue for the latter. Allegations involving monetary dishonesty and corruption at regulated lending institutions is serious at a prima facie level. Clinton employed transcendence successfully in this scandal.

Chapter Seven

That Woman: The Lewinsky Affair

This chapter will examine Clinton's discourse subsequent to allegations that he had engaged in an improper sexual relationship with White House intern Monica Lewinsky. Above and beyond the moral impropriety involved were accusations that Clinton may have committed perjury, suborned perjury, and obstructed justice in connection with the alleged affair. This blossomed into an impeachment inquiry, indicating the gravity of these charges.

The accusations will be detailed, followed by an analysis of Clinton's remarks in each of his major responses to the allegations. Finally, an evaluation of his entire set of discourse will be offered, employing external data as well as internal rhetorical standards.

THE PERSUASIVE ATTACK

In January 1998, Whitewater Special Counsel Kenneth Starr requested and received permission from Attorney General Janet Reno to expand his investigation. The issue at hand was whether Clinton had engaged in an inappropriate sexual relationship with White House intern Monica Lewinsky and lied about that relationship in a legal deposition with Paula Jones' attorneys. Moreover, it was alleged that Clinton and/or his friend Vernon Jordan had suborned perjury by encouraging Lewinsky to lie about the affair under oath. Moreover, Starr charged that Clinton may have obstructed justice by requesting the return of gifts he allegedly gave Lewinsky (Froomkin, 1998a).

The *New York Times* editorial page described the seriousness of the matter:

> It is not the legality of anyone's sexual behavior that is at issue here. The legal questions before Mr. Starr are obstruction of justice, perjury and suborning of perjury. By press accounts, Ms. Reno took them seriously enough to deliberate only 24 hours before asking a federal court to expand Mr. Starr's mandate, even though she had the right under the Independent Counsel Act to inform the court that such an expansion was not warranted. (Tell the full story, 1998, p. A20)

Legal analyst Stuart Taylor (1998) concurred with the gravity of the situation: "If Starr can show that Clinton had sexual relations with Monica Lewinsky and tried to get her to make false denials under oath, then Clinton would be in jeopardy of possible impeachment, eventual criminal prosecution, or both" (p. 48). Clearly, much was at stake.

Both of these descriptions detailed how Clinton needed to defend himself from accusations that he (1) committed adultery, (2) lied under oath, (3) encouraged others to lie under oath, and (4) obstructed justice. Notably, three of the four accusations constitute legal violations, not merely moral offenses.

THE PERSUASIVE DEFENSE

Benoit's (1995a) method will be applied to Clinton's discourse in two subsets: (1) his initial January 1998 statements on the matter to interviewers in *Roll Call* and *The News Hour* as well as statements made after a photo opportunity with the After-School Program; and (2) Clinton's August 17, 1998, address to the nation and September 11, 1998, remarks at the White House Prayer Breakfast. The discourse is divided as such for two obvious reasons. First, the rhetorical artifacts have a temporal separation of eight months. Second, they are radically different in their approach to the underlying allegations.

The First Wave: Total Denial

In the first wave of discourse Clinton relied primarily on denial, followed by bolstering and transcendence. These strategies will be discussed in that order.

Denial

Clinton denied wrongdoing on several occasions. On some occasions he chose merely to deny any sexual escapades. For instance, when pressed for his definition of an improper relationship, he denied wrongdoing again: "Well, I think you know what it means. It means that there is not a sexual relationship, an improper sexual relationship, or any other kind of improper relationship" (Clinton, 1998a). He denied sexual impropriety again: "Well, let me say, the relationship was not improper, and I think that's important enough to say . . . it is not an improper relationship and I know what the word means" (Clinton, 1998b). Moreover, in order to remove any ambiguity about the nature of the contact, Clinton was asked if the relationship was in any way sexual, to which he replied: "The relationship was not sexual. And I know what you mean, and the answer is no" (Clinton, 1998b). In short, his denial was unequivocal. Finally, Clinton made the now infamous "finger-wagging" denial: "But I want to say one thing to the American people. I want you to listen to me. I'm going to say this again. I did not have sexual relations with that woman, Miss Lewinsky" (Clinton, 1998c). In other words, Clinton's denial was complete.

On other occasions, he denied encouraging illegal testimony. For instance, when asked by Jim Lehrer whether Clinton had suborned perjury by asking Monica Lewinsky to falsely deny under oath having had an affair with him, Clinton replied: "That is not true. That is not true. I did not ask anyone to tell anything other than the truth. There is no improper relationship" (Clinton, 1998b). This served the dual purpose of denying an affair with Lewinsky while also denying subornation of perjury, an impeachable offense.

Clinton chose to deny categorically any legal impropriety, including subornation of perjury. For instance, consider his direct dismissal of the allegations:

> I did not urge anyone to say anything that was untrue. I did not urge anyone to say anything that was untrue. That's my statement to you. And beyond that, I think it's very important that we let the investigation take its course. But I want you to know that that is my clear position. I didn't ask anyone to go in there and say something that's not true. (Clinton, 1998a)

This statement explicitly denied legal wrongdoing. He denied subornation of perjury again when Lehrer asked if Clinton directed his friend Vernon Jordan to aid in quieting Lewinsky with a job in New York City:

I absolutely did not do that. I can tell you I did not do that. I did not do that. He is in no way involved in trying to get anybody to say anything that's not true at my request. I didn't do that. (Clinton, 1998b)

Again, his denial of legal misfeasance was vehement.

He repeated the denial again later that afternoon: "I made it very clear that the allegations are not true. I didn't ask anybody not to tell the truth" (Clinton, 1998a). Moreover, just days after the initial denial, he sought to put the issue to rest: "I never told anybody to lie. Not a single time—never. These allegations are false" (Clinton, 1998c). In short, these examples of denial show how Clinton denied both sexual impropriety and legal wrongdoing immediately after the Lewinsky scandal broke.

Bolstering

Clinton used the bolstering strategy to portray himself as virtuous despite the allegations. For instance, he extolled his cooperative nature:

We are doing our best to cooperate here, but we don't know much yet. And that's all I can say now. What I'm trying to do is to contain my natural impulses and get back to work. I think it's important that we cooperate. I will cooperate. (Clinton, 1998b)

Here, Clinton portrayed himself as cooperative with the investigation. Such cooperation could surely be viewed positively and may well have implied to some that he had nothing to hide.

He stressed his willingness to cooperate again: "I'm going to cooperate . . . and I will be vigorous about it" (Clinton, 1998b). Moreover, he referred to past investigations to augment his strategy: "I'll do my best to cooperate with this, just as I have through every other issue that's come up over the last several years" (Clinton, 1998b). In other words, Clinton implied that he would employ his usual admirable character in cooperating with the investigators.

He offered yet another form of bolstering when he described how he would spend the upcoming days following the investigation: "I'm just going to go back to work and do the best I can" (Clinton, 1998a). This statement bolstered Clinton's fortitude and strength in the face of adversity. These examples all demonstrate how Clinton used bolstering to present himself in a positive light despite the accusations at hand.

Transcendence

The final strategy Clinton used during the first phase of his image repair efforts was transcendence. He attempted to place the sordid allegations against him in the context of his presidential duties. For instance, after assuring Jim Lehrer that he would cooperate with the investigation, he pointed to his duties: "But I want to focus on the work at hand" (Clinton, 1998b), implying that the work at hand was more important. He made a similar statement after agreeing that he would cooperate just as he had always done: "But I have got to get back to work . . . I've got to go on with the work of the country. I got hired to help the rest of the American people" (Clinton, 1998b). These statements portrayed the allegations as unimportant compared to his official obligations.

Clinton forcefully reiterated this point during his now infamous remarks at the After-School Program. Coupled with his forceful denial he declared, "And I need to go back to work for the American people" (Clinton, 1998c). More precisely, he also offered an explanation of what he hoped to accomplish:

> And we've got a lot to do. I'm going to give them [Congress] the first balanced budget three years ahead of time, and a great child care initiative, and an important Medicare initiative. We've got a Medicare commission meeting. (Clinton, 1998a)

Here, Clinton detailed the things he needed to tend to which were, he would argue, more important than the Lewinsky matter.

All of the above provide examples of transcendence. In some instances, Clinton merely claimed that there were more important things to focus on. However, he also provided details of specific initiatives he would like to be addressing rather than the scandal in question.

The Second Wave: Partial Concession

Before analyzing the second wave of defense, the reader should note that the evidence of wrongdoing had been substantially augmented. Monica Lewinsky produced a dress for prosecutors which she claimed was soiled with Clinton's semen (presumably spilled on the dress during sexual activity). The FBI was having the stain analyzed to determine whether it matched Clinton genetically.

In the second wave, Clinton made two addresses. They were similar insofar as they both recognized that he had committed adulterous behavior and had been deceitful toward the public. However, they were different insofar as one speech was defiant while the other was more conciliatory. In the August 17, 1998, address to the nation, Clinton relied primarily on attack accuser and transcendence, but also engaged in mortification, denial, bolstering, corrective action, good intentions, and minimization. In the September 11, 1998, White House Prayer Breakfast he relied most on mortification and corrective action, followed by transcendence, differentiation, bolstering, and attack accuser. Because the strategies stressed in the two speeches are so radically different, they merit subsections in this analysis.

August 17, 1998

Clinton's August 17, 1998, speech was greatly anticipated because it came the evening following his testimony in front of the grand jury assembled for the Whitewater investigation. He engaged primarily in attack accuser and transcendence, but used other strategies as well.

Attack Accuser. Clinton attacked his accusers on multiple occasions. For instance, he took aim at the independent counsel directly: "In addition, I had real and serious concerns about an independent counsel investigation that began with private business dealings 20 years ago" (Clinton, 1998d). This statement surely sought to attack the investigation as worthy of contempt since it was allegedly irrelevant to the initial questions of wrongdoing. Clinton continued with his attack on Starr: "The independent counsel investigation moved on to my staff and friends, then into my private life. And now the investigation itself is under investigation" (Clinton, 1998d). Moreover, Clinton attacked the general character of the investigation: "This has gone on too long, cost too much and hurt too many innocent people" (Clinton, 1998d). As such, Clinton attacked Starr's investigation as an expensive, overreaching menace.

Perhaps his most incriminating attack came in the form of a call for privacy: "It is time to stop the pursuit of personal destruction and the prying into private lives" (Clinton, 1998d). With this statement, Clinton attacked Starr implicitly by accusing him of being interested in "personal destruction," rather than a proper investigation. He attacked the solicitors in the case where he allegedly lied under oath: "The fact that these questions were being asked in a politically inspired lawsuit . . . was a consideration too" (Clinton, 1998d). Here, Clinton attacked the motives of Jones' attorneys, the ones responsible for asking the questions in the first place. The above examples each demonstrate how he attacked his accusers as part of his persuasive defense.

Transcendence. Clinton also relied on transcendence to a great extent. He argued for two aspects of transcendence: (1) that the matter was private and

(2) that official business was more important. For instance, Clinton argued that the matter was too private for discussion: "It is private, and I intend to reclaim my family life for my family. It's nobody's business but ours" (Clinton, 1998d). In other words, Clinton claimed his private sphere was off-limits to inquiry. He argued that since the allegations at hand were irrelevant to his presidency, they were beyond any public scrutiny or concern.

He called for the nation to get past the issue: "Now it is time—in fact, it is past time to move on" (Clinton, 1998d). In other words, he argued, there were more important things to do and the country should not delay in addressing the issues while forgetting this unfortunate episode. He hinted at specifics: "We have important work to do—real opportunities to seize, real problems to solve, real security matters to face" (Clinton, 1998d). As the speech came only days after the bombing of American embassies in the Sudan and Tanzania, one could surely understand the president's statement as a reference to fighting terrorism directed at Americans.

Finally, he closed by asking the audience to understand a larger context:

And so tonight, I ask you to turn away from the spectacle of the past seven months, to repair the fabric of our national discourse, and to return our attention to all the challenges and all the promise of the next American century. (Clinton, 1998d)

After this, the president wished the country a good night, hoping they would perceive the whole scandal as unimportant to the nation's future. These examples all show how Clinton used transcendence in the address.

Mortification. The speech, touted beforehand as a "mea culpa," used mortification, but to a lesser degree than attack accuser and transcendence. For instance, Clinton confessed to the alleged affair with Lewinsky:

Indeed, I did have a relationship with Miss Lewinsky that was not appropriate. In fact, it was wrong. It constituted a critical lapse in judgment and a personal failure on my part for which I am solely and completely responsible. (Clinton, 1998d)

In short, Clinton admitted to an inappropriate (but, as it turned out, not necessarily sexual) relationship with the former White House intern. Moreover, he claimed responsibility for the misdeed.

Next, he moved on to mortification over his past dissembling on the matter: "I know that my public comments and my silence about this matter gave a false impression. I misled people, including even my wife. I deeply regret that" (Clinton, 1998d). Here, Clinton admitted to lying about the matter to the country and his wife.

Finally, he communicated his supposed willingness to take responsibility for the ugly incident: "I take responsibility for my part in all of this. That is all I can do" (Clinton, 1998d). In short, though he did not actually utter the word "sorry," it is implied that he feels sorrow over the pain the country has felt due to "his" part in the controversy. The preceding examples show how Clinton engaged in mortification.

Denial. Clinton used denial to respond to other allegations. Most notably, he denied any legal wrongdoing: "While my answers were legally accurate, I did not offer any information" (Clinton, 1998d). By pointing to the legal accuracy of his statements, he denied perjury outright. One could argue that he was differentiating perjury from something else, but that "something else" was never defined in this utterance. As such, the statement is best understood as denial.

He addressed the question of whether he had encouraged people to obstruct justice: "I told the grand jury today and I say to you now that at no time did I ask anyone to lie, to hide or destroy evidence or to take any other unlawful action" (Clinton, 1998d). Both of these statements illustrate Clinton's use of denial in the address.

Corrective action. Clinton promised corrective action, albeit not specifically: "I must put it right, and I am prepared to do whatever it takes to do so" (Clinton, 1998d). In short, he promised to make some unnamed amends.

He went on to augment that promise: "Nothing is more important to me [than his family] personally" (Clinton, 1998d). In other words, his assurance that he would correct the situation should be believed.

Good intentions. Clinton used the good intentions strategy to explain his motivation for lying: "I can only tell you I was motivated by many factors. First by a desire to protect myself from the embarrassment of my own conduct. I was also very concerned about protecting my family" (Clinton, 1998d). While trying to protect oneself from embarrassment might not qualify as a good intention, protecting one's family certainly does. Regardless, claiming that his motivations were helpful, and not vindictive, Clinton attempted to escape some of the blame for lying.

Minimization. Clinton minimized his dishonesty in the Jones deposition in the course of an attack described earlier in this chapter: "The fact that these questions were being asked in a politically inspired lawsuit, which since has been dismissed, was a consideration, too" (Clinton, 1998d). In short, since the testimony took place in a suit that had been dismissed (though one should note it was *not* dismissed at the time), the infraction was not as offensive as it might have been in a more "legitimate" case. One should note that the minimization is accomplished through an attack on the accuser, allegedly a purveyor of tainted justice.

The above strategies all demonstrate how Clinton sought to repair his image during his August 17, 1998, address to the nation. He relied primarily on attack accuser and transcendence, but used other strategies as well.

September 11, 1998

While similar in some regards to the August address, Clinton's September 11, 1998, speech at the White House Prayer Breakfast showed more contrition. He engaged overwhelmingly in mortification and corrective action in this message. However, he also used transcendence, differentiation, bolstering, and attack accuser to a much lesser degree.

Mortification. As previously mentioned, Clinton engaged in much more mortification in this speech than in the previous one. In fact, he noted this himself: "I agree with those who have said that in my first statement after I testified I was not contrite enough. I don't think there is a fancy way to say that I have sinned" (Clinton, 1998e). In short, he expressed contrition over not expressing enough contrition. He continued with the theme:

> It is important to me that everybody who has been hurt know that the sorrow I feel is genuine: first and most important, my family; also my friends, my staff, my cabinet, Monica Lewinsky and her family, and the American people. I have asked all for their forgiveness. (Clinton, 1998e)

Here, Clinton attempted to convey to those who suffered from his dishonesty that he felt genuine sorrow. He explicitly listed several victims of his dishonesty and explictly said he had asked for their forgiveness.

Another example of mortification dwelled on his need for spiritual absolution:

> I ask you to share my prayer that God will search me and know my heart, try me and know my anxious thoughts, see if there is any hurtfulness in me, and lead me toward the life everlasting. I ask that God give me a clean heart, let me walk by faith and not sight. (Clinton, 1998e)

His request for "a clean heart" underscored his sorrow over his soiled soul. He continued in prayer:

I ask once again to be able to love my neighbor—all my neighbors—as my self, to be an instrument of God's peace; to let the words
of my mouth and the meditations of my heart and, in the end, the work
of my hands, be pleasing. (Clinton, 1998e)

As such, it is clear that Clinton was verbally admitting to falling short of
God's standards of love of neighbor. Moreover, he wanted to be cleansed so
he could "once again" love his neighbors.

Clinton also used a unique form of mortification via his reading an ex-
cerpt from the Yom Kippur liturgy, "Gates of Repentance." He quoted the
text verbatim:

Now is the time for turning. The leaves are beginning to turn from
green to red to orange. The birds are beginning to turn and are heading
once more toward the south. The animals are beginning to turn to stor-
ing their food for winter. For leaves, birds and animals, turning comes
instinctively. But for us, turning does not come so easily. It takes an
act of will for us to make a turn. It means breaking old habits. It means
admitting that we have been wrong, and this is never easy. (Clinton,
1998e)

Clinton appeared to be using the substance of that text to proxy another
statement of regret for his actions. Basically, he used the text to admit
wrongdoing and articulate the heaviness of heart which it accompanies.
The preceding examples demonstrate Clinton's mortification in this
speech.

Corrective Action. Of course, when a party admits to committing a misdeed, one might expect some promise to avoid its repetition. Clinton provided multiple examples. For instance, he outlined two necessary
components for healing:

I believe that to be forgiven, more than sorrow is required—at least
two more things. First, genuine repentance—a determination to
change and to repair breaches of my own making. I have repented.
Second, what my Bible calls a "broken spirit"; an understanding that I
must have God's help to be the person that I want to be; a willingness
to give the very forgiveness that I seek; a renunciation of the pride and
anger which cloud judgment, lead people to excuse and compare and
to blame and complain. (Clinton, 1998e)

The various ways of describing contrition were notable here. He spoke of the need for "genuine repentance," "a determination to change and repair breaches," and his "renunciation of pride and anger." Adopting these in combination, he would be the person he wanted to become.

He repeated his plans later in the speech: "And if my repentance is genuine and sustained, and if I can maintain both a broken spirit and a strong heart, then good can come of this for our country as well as for me and my family" (Clinton, 1998e). Again, he vaguely referred to corrective action intended to prevent future impropriety.

Another source of corrective action could be found in the healing power of God: "The children of this country can learn in a profound way that integrity is important and selfishness is wrong, but God can change us and make us strong at the broken places" (Clinton, 1998e). In short, he argued that divine intervention could aid and help alter people, including himself. These examples show how Clinton used the promises of corrective action to repair his image.

Transcendence. Though this speech featured mortification and corrective action overwhelmingly, Clinton also used transcendence. For instance, he used transcendence on one occasion to temper his mortification: "Though I cannot move beyond or forget this—indeed, I must always keep it as a caution light in my life—it is very important that our nation move forward" (Clinton, 1998e). In short, the issues facing the nation were important. Moreover, Clinton said that in spite of his regret over his behavior, the country's interests should come before attendance to his shortcomings. This example demonstrates how Clinton used transcendence in his verbal defense discourse.

Bolstering. Clinton turned a would-be expression of thanks into an acclamation of his character:

> I am very grateful for the many, many people—clergy and ordinary citizens alike—who have written me with wise counsel. I am profoundly grateful for the support of so many Americans who somehow through it all seem to still know that I care about them a great deal, that I care about their problems and their dreams. (Clinton, 1998e)

In other words, he argued that he still had the support of many because of his commitment to their defining (though unspecified) causes or wishes. People knew he cared about them. This example shows how Clinton used bolstering in his discourse.

Attack accuser. Clinton continued with his reference to those who still supported him while attacking his accuser: "I am grateful for those who have stood by me and who say that in this case and many others, the bounds of the presidency have been excessively and unwisely invaded" (Clinton, 1998e). This example shows that Clinton chose not to cease criticizing his accusers altogether. However, one should notice that this attack was indirect, where Clinton referred to the others who thought his privacy had been invaded.

Differentiation. Finally, Clinton used differentiation on only one occasion, although that instance is quite notable. In the course of apologizing for his misdeeds, he made the distinction between his moral shortcomings and his presumed legal purity: "I will instruct my lawyers to mount a vigorous defense, using all available appropriate arguments. But, legal language must not obscure the fact that I have done wrong" (Clinton, 1998e). In other words, Clinton argued that his moral wrongdoing was not tantamount to legal wrongdoing and that he would make such legal arguments. This example illustrates how Clinton used differentiation in an important context.

During his White House Prayer Breakfast speech, Clinton engaged primarily in mortification and corrective action. However, he also used transcendence, attack accuser, bolstering, and differentiation in his discourse.

EVALUATION

Both phases of Clinton's discourse in the Monica Lewinsky matter will be evaluated by internal and external criteria. First, it will be examined for internal consistency and plausibility. Second, external data from opinion articles in the *New York Times* as well as public opinion data will be considered in its assessment.

First Phase

Clinton's discourse in the first phase will be evaluated by two criteria. First, it will be assessed for internal cogency. Second, commentary from the *New York Times* and public polling data will provide a measure of external, public reaction.

Internal Consistency and Plausibility

Clinton's initial discourse concerning the scandal was probably persuasive to different degrees with different groups. With partisan supporters, he was probably either believed or supported in spite of nonbelief. Likewise, partisan opponents were probably unpersuadable.

A strong denial combined with assertions that his presidency was robust and that the matter was irrelevant to the nation's business could bring an end to the matter. Surely, if Clinton could convince the persuadable public that he performed no misdeed, then his discourse would be successful. When the allegations of adultery, perjury, and suborning perjury first surfaced, there was only limited evidence of the deeds: tape-recorded conversations of a former White House intern talking about her alleged affair with Clinton with a former White House employee. There was merely evidence of claim of an affair, not physical evidence of an affair. Of course, Clinton's leaked testimony in the Paula Jones case revealed that President Clinton admitted to an affair with Gennifer Flowers. This discovery may have reduced Clinton's credibility. However, denial was a plausible (if not entirely believable) strategy as long as conclusive proof was lacking.

Bolstering was probably effective in this instance. He made reference both to his alleged cooperation with the investigation and his achievements as president. This would surely lead the persuadable portion of his audience to view him more favorably in general.

Finally, transcendence was a particularly wise choice of strategies. Since Clinton was presiding over an excellent economy and a relatively content nation, his claim that he needed to deal with important national issues rather than minor, scandalous distractions would be well received.

The combination of denial and transcendence was particularly effective. For those who believed the denials, his image was repaired. For those who doubted his denial, transcendence may have adequately defined the misdeed as irrelevant to his presidency. Only those people who doubted the denial and did not subscribe to the transcendency would be unpersuaded. Luckily for Clinton, these people were in the minority.

Polling Data

In terms of public opinion polls, Clinton's image repair received a mixed reaction. In general, the public was split over his handling of the issue. Forty percent believed that Clinton's handling of the issue made his situation better, while 39 percent believed it made the situation worse (Public Opinion Online, 1998a).

However, the more specific the polls became, the more favorable his situation became in public reaction. For instance, 61 percent of the public came to believe that the Lewinsky matter was a personal issue for Clinton while only 31 percent thought it was a reflection on his job as president (Public Opinion Online, 1998a). In other words, the public adopted Clinton's two transcendent arguments: (1) there were concerns more pressing than this scandal, and (2) the matter was private.

Moreover, while only 18 percent of the public thought Clinton was being entirely truthful, only 38 percent thought he was hiding something that the

public needed to know about (Public Opinion Online, 1998a). This reinforced the idea that Clinton's problems were not widely perceived as relevant to his performance in office, supporting his transcendency claim again.

Finally, fully 60 percent of those polled believed that the matter posed no
interference with Clinton's performance in office (Public Opinion Online,
1998a). This echoed Clinton's earlier bolstering that he would remain un-
distracted from his duties.

Commentary

Commentary in the *New York Times* indicated that Clinton's discourse
had a mixed reception. The paper editorialized:

> The term "carefully worded" has appeared in almost every descrip-
> tion of President Clinton's denials of sexual involvement with
> Monica Lewinsky. Other words that could as easily be applied are
> cryptic, partial and insufficient. . . . This approach, which depends so
> heavily on omission and factual elision, is appropriate to people who
> believe themselves to be targets of a criminal investigation. But it is
> not sufficient for Mr. Clinton's other role as leader of the nation. (Tell
> the full story, 1998, p. A20)

This comment clearly indicated dissatisfaction with Clinton's legalistic,
unforthcoming statements. The paper wondered publicly whether Clinton
would muster the will to put the issue to rest with a proper explanation:

> The optimistic citizen can pray for Mr. Clinton to break free of the en-
> tangling advice of his lawyers and embrace the central Presidential
> task of shaping the nation's political climate. . . . A worried nation is
> waiting to see what steps President Clinton takes toward a steadier
> balance. (State of the presidency, 1998, p. 14)

In short, the paper criticized Clinton for speaking more legalistically than
presidentially.

Maureen Dowd summarized her opinion of the president's discourse,
showing incredulity at the public's outrage. The public should not be upset
by Clinton's lies, she argued, because they knew about his character when
they elected him. She opined: "The President and his minions dissembling
and splitting hairs and playing semantic games and taking forever to find
the documents until our attention wanders? *Knew that*" (Dowd, 1998a, p.
15). Her sarcasm illustrated that she disapproved of Clinton's evasive

speech even though it was to be expected of him. Columnist Bob Herbert agreed:

> Mr. Clinton is being urged to come clean, to address the nation and tell the entire truth. But that raises another question. After so many years of his cheap lies and easy deceptions, why should anyone ever believe Bill Clinton? (1998a, p. 15)

Herbert certainly did not laud Clinton's speech. Moreover, he argued that given Clinton's track record people would have trouble believing him at all.

Thomas Friedman was also unimpressed by the president's evasive speech:

> Yes, I know we don't know the full story. I know we haven't heard the President's full disclosure. But I've heard enough non-denial denials to know that whether this was an "emotional" relationship, a "special" relationship, a "not proper" relationship or some sort of backroom clothes-on relationship, the President was involved with someone in a way he never should have been and by doing so he has let down all of those who believed, if not in him personally, in the policies he was elected to implement. (1998, p. A19)

Considering that Dowd, Herbert and Friedman were Clinton supporters, their criticisms were even more indicting.

Though none of the articles explicitly approved of Clinton's actions or discourse, he did have some defenders. Janna Malamud Smith asked readers to consider dropping the whole issue: "My own feeling is that short of seriously criminal behavior (rape, child molestation, incest) we ought to send all politicians for a medical exam, rule out serious illness, insanity or severe addiction, and leave the rest alone" (1998, p. A19). In short, Smith defended Clinton by trying to remove the allegations from the public agenda of important issues. Columnist Anthony Lewis also took issue with the sexual nature of the investigation: "We do not want . . . prosecutors looking into the sex lives of presidents. We should not have tawdry tales of their investigations filling our newspapers and television screens" (1998, p. A19). Thus, Lewis offered defensive cover for the president.

Clinton also received the support of letter writers. For instance, Roger Kirby wrote:

> Of course, rational people do not endorse rampant adultery or perjury. But do we really want to be the sort of people who would consume a

young woman's life in the less than likely prospect that a lame-duck
President could be removed from office less than two years before the
end of his term? (1998, p. A14)

Again, a Clinton supporter claimed that the matter was not fit for public interest. On balance, however, one must conclude that the commentary on
Clinton's behavior does not support a positive evaluation of his image repair discourse. Most articles were critical of Clinton in general. Moreover,
even those who supported him by adopting his transcendence arguments
wrote as though they assumed his denial of adultery was false (if not the denials of perjury and suborning perjury).

Second Phase

The second phase of Clinton's discourse will also be evaluated by two
criteria. First, the internal consistency and plausibility of the arguments will
be considered. Second, external reaction found in the *New York Times* and
public polling data will be considered. Clinton's discourse in the second
phase can be evaluated in two sections. The first will address the disastrous
August 17, 1998, address to the nation. The second will consider his more
appropriate September 11, 1998, speech at the White House Prayer Breakfast.

August 17, 1998

Internal Consistency and Plausibility. Clinton's discourse in the second
phase was markedly less effective. His August 17, 1998, address to the nation relied primarily on attack accuser and transcendence. The transcendence strategy had the potential to be effective as it asked Americans to
place his admitted misdeeds in the context of arguably more important matters. Moreover, as the evaluation of the first phase demonstrated, the public
considered the matter a private concern. Clinton erred when he decided to
anchor his message with an attack on special counsel Starr. The speech was
given on the very same day that Clinton admitted in grand jury testimony
that he had an inappropriate relationship with Lewinsky, a relationship he
had vehemently denied on multiple public occasions. Clinton had
"wagged" his finger at the American people, chastising them for giving cre-
dence to the allegations of infidelity. He was now admitting his deceit. As
such, the speech should have been replete with mortification. Instead, it
functioned to attack more than to apologize. Certainly, part of the speech
could have served to attack and transcend, but his failure to mortify adequately was inappropriate.

Additionally, his assertion that his answers in the Jones deposition were "legally accurate," was ill-chosen for repairing his image, although it may have aided his legal case. Of course, his discourse on this night was probably oriented toward two goals: (1) repairing his reputation and (2) avoiding legal problems that might prompt his ouster. However, it was not persuasive for Clinton to "split hairs" over the meaning of sexual relations. It made him appear decidedly less contrite and more evasive and defiant in front of the two-thirds of all adult Americans who watched the speech.

Polling Data. Public reaction to the speech revealed two major findings: (1) that the public viewed Clinton less favorably, however, (2) his lack of personal favorability did not overwhelmingly bother the public (Poll, August 17, 1998). A CNN/USA Today/Gallup poll conducted immediately following the speech indicated that Clinton's job performance approval remained at a 62 percent favorability rating. Additionally, by a margin of 65 percent to 31 percent, most Americans thought Clinton's testimony and subsequent speech should have ended the matter. Moreover, a 53 percent majority were satisfied with his speech, and 63 percent thought the issue was a private matter (Poll, August 17, 1998).

Even more to Clinton's credit, 44 percent of those polled placed blame for the incidents on Starr while only 39 percent blamed Clinton (Polls show job approval, August 18, 1998). This indicates that Clinton's attacks on Starr were probably effective, if not appropriate.

However, not all of the data reflected favorably on Clinton. The same survey showed that more people had an unfavorable opinion of Clinton (48 percent) than a favorable (40 percent) opinion. Still, strong majorities opposed both impeachment (69 percent) and resignation (72 percent), in spite of the fact that the majority (48 percent) believed he broke the law (Poll, August 17, 1998).

Commentary. Commentary from the *New York Times* corroborated this assessment. That paper editorialized:

> The moment the 42nd President walked into the Map Room he was in a confrontation with a force far more insidious than Kenneth Starr, the independent counsel. In that hallowed room, Mr. Clinton was also confronting the habit that has driven—and haunted—his political career in an almost addictive way. His habit of stonewalling, of misleading by omission or concealment or fabrication or failure of memory has been the source of virtually all this Administration's troubles. (Betrayal, 1998, p. A30)

This sentiment took Clinton to task for his inability to be truthful and judged that flaw as more perilous to Clinton than even an investigation of his conduct. The same editorial board opined again:

> President Clinton has failed that simple test [trustworthiness, loyalty, and judgment] abjectly, not merely with undignified private behavior in a revered place, but with his cavalier response to public concern. That is why the cursory speech he made before departing on vacation probably did him more harm than good. (Betrayal, 1998, p. A30)

This editorial clearly labels the speech as unsuccessful, a merely "cursory" response to a profound loss of trust by the public.

Dowd took issue with Clinton's portrayal of the scandal as primarily personal:

> Rather than tell the truth about a cheesy office affair seven months ago, he dragged Washington and America into a stupid, phony war. It's not a war about ideology or principles or privacy rights, although the Clintons like to cast it that way. It's a war about how much Bill Clinton can get away with and still keep our affection. He's constantly testing the limits of our love. (1998c, A29)

Dowd's appraisal takes issue with Clinton's assertions that the matter was private and that the matter was beyond public scrutiny. This sentiment is directly at odds with Clinton's discourse.

Columnist Bob Herbert, thinking that Clinton would have been forgiven had he come clean, expressed disappointment:

> He went on television and offered defiance where so many had hoped to see contrition. He never admitted that he had lied at all. He never apologized. And he angrily attacked Kenneth Starr, the Whitewater independent counsel. (1998c, p. A23)

Here, Herbert appeared to be arguing that mortification would have been appropriate, and that to attack the accuser was misplaced in this context. Moreover, he thought the speech was particularly foolish given Senate Judiciary chairman Orrin Hatch's promise that impeachment would not happen if Clinton were fully honest with the grand jury.

Letters to the editor were also largely unfavorable for Clinton. For instance, Alan Rivers wrote, "Bill Clinton's attempt to make Kenneth W.

Starr the villain makes his apology rather hollow" (1998, p. A30). Other critical letters were plentiful.

Clinton's defenders were few. A letter from English parliament member Nick Palmer pointed to Clinton's virtues as a leader: "The allies of the United States recognize Mr. Clinton's strengths and want to work with him in the remaining years of office on issues as diverse as the Japanese and Russian crises, the embassy bombings and the long-term challenges of global warming" (1998, p. A28). Tamara Baker provided cover for Clinton by attacking the Republicans: "The public agrees with President Clinton: the Lewinsky matter should end here. But both Mr. Clinton and the public know that Republicans won't let it die" (1998, p. A24). Notably, neither of these letters defended Clinton's discourse. They merely expressed general support for him.

Only Adrienne Aurichio's letter defended Clinton's decision not to apologize:

Ms. Lewinsky may have been a 21–year-old intern, but she was also a sexually mature young woman who entered into a relationship with another woman's husband, who happened to be the President. When you play that game, you don't get apologies. (1998, p. A14)

This letter indicated that an apology (at least to Lewinsky) was not called for.

All of this data complicates how this speech should be evaluated. The vast majority of columnists and writers of letters to the editor condemned his actions and subsequent image repair as inappropriate. A majority of those polled had unfavorable views of Clinton as a person. Certainly his personal image suffered. Yet, the same people: (1) wanted Clinton to remain in office; (2) thought the matter was private; (3) blamed Starr more than Clinton; (4) thought the testimony and speech should end the matter; and (5) were satisfied with Clinton's speech. This data supports the conclusion that the columnists, letter writers, and this rhetorical critic were largely out of touch with popular sentiment in this matter.

I conclude that this speech should receive a mixed evaluation. Clinton had lied about this matter to the country for eight months. Only after incontrovertible, physical evidence of his misdeed was produced did he admit to lying. Moreover, his "mea culpa" speech functioned more to attack his accusers than to offer the mortification that was clearly necessary after such inexcusable behavior. Attacking Starr was an inappropriate choice in this particular speech, which should have been wholly contrite. Admittedly, Clinton's attacks on Starr may have been effective as Starr had an unfavorability rating of 56 percent (Public Opinion Online, 1998b). However, one could plausibly argue that his sequence of actions (denial, attacking, transcending, reluctantly admitting, attacking, transcending) indicated that he was not really contrite about the affair, only sorry that he was caught. As such, his scarcity of mortification was further exaggerated.

The strategy that was most effective (indeed, has been effective throughout) was transcendence. Even when the public thought Clinton was lying, they agreed with his argument that the matters were both personal and irrelevant.

Clinton prolonged the matter by his persistence in deceit. His personal rating plummeted 20 percent overnight. The fact that the vast majority opposed impeachment or resignation may serve only as a barometer of public contentment at the time or perhaps a general agreement with Clinton's policies. However, these numbers may also indicate agreement with Clinton's transcendence.

September 11, 1998

Internal Consistency and Plausibility. Clinton's speech at the White House Prayer Breakfast was much more appropriate than his address to the nation. First, it focused on the mortification appropriate when someone has been found guilty of (or admitted to) a serious misdeed. Second, corrective action designed to prevent the recurrence of such misdeeds was represented as well. These were Clinton's two primary strategies in the address.

Clinton also nominally used transcendence, bolstering, differentiation, and attack accuser. Transcendence was appropriate for the same reason throughout the scandal. It attempted to turn the public's attention to larger issues. Bolstering was also appropriate since it merely asked people to consider his virtues alongside his vices.

However, differentiation and attack accuser were less appropriate. One might readily agree that Clinton had two different rhetorical purposes: (1) repairing image, and (2) avoiding legal/official punishment. However, his public persistence in "splitting hairs" over the legal accuracy of his deceptive testimony risked mitigating his ability to be perceived as contrite. Moreover, his continued attack on Kenneth Starr, while effective in demonizing Starr, could also reduce the effectiveness of his professed contrition. However, the focus on mortification in this speech mitigated that hazard.

Polling Data. Public opinion polling also showed that the public had mixed feelings. In the week following the Prayer Breakfast, 59 percent of those polled wanted Clinton censured by Congress and 35 percent wanted him to resign, but only 30 percent wanted him impeached, a slight tick down from 31 percent following the August 17th speech. On top of all this, his approval rating for job performance ticked up a percentage point to 63 percent (Poll, 1998). In other words, most Americans were angry with the president to some degree, but still wanted him in office. Transcendence had been effective all along for Clinton. His added mortification and corrective action in this address may have helped him (and the country) achieve some moral, if not political, closure on the matter.

Commentary. Once again, commentary in the *New York Times* presented a mixed reaction. Clinton received more support from columnists. For instance, Elliot Richardson argued that impeachment might be an excessive punishment:

> Removing Mr. Clinton from office might well be an excessive penalty given the noncriminal [sic], nonofficial [sic] character of his initial offense as well as this society's disposition to cloak sexual behavior from public exposure. (1998, p. A27)

In short, Richardson tried to defend Clinton from the worst case scenario of impeachment.

Katie Roiphe took Clinton's defense one step further by portraying him as the victim of Lewinsky:

> When she was frustrated with the progress of her job search she used her personal power over the President to get results: she herself says that she threatened him with disclosure to hasten the process. (1998, p. A31)

This statement clearly conveys empathy for Clinton in the matter.

Moreover, the most supportive sentiments came from letters to the editor. Susan Eisner thought that the independent counsel's report to Congress would help Clinton:

> The Starr report may turn out to be President Clinton's best friend. Its detail makes clear that all is told; its contents may reinforce sympathetic public opinion that Bill Clinton is a vulnerable human being, not one who has committed high crimes and misdemeanors. (1998, p. A26)

In short, Clinton's admissions could be seen as a plus. George Wozniak also provided moral support as he pointed to Lewinsky's role in these events:

> Her behavior toward the President was apparently aggressive, quite explicit and implicit in nature. Perhaps it is time that Ms. Lewinsky publicly apologize for her behavior toward the President, his wife and daughter, and to the American people. (1998, p. A30)

Here again, Clinton was portrayed as the victim. He was more than simply forgiven. He was pitied.

Of course, there were some critical letters as well. Timothy McManus believed Clinton's actions merited removal:

> Monica S. Lewinsky was a willing participant in her dalliance with the President. However, that does not excuse Mr. Clinton from manipulating a vulnerable employee. His conduct would draw an outcry for his removal if he were a manager at any public company. (1998, p. A30)

Similarly, Richard Foster believed that Clinton should be held accountable:

> Mr. Clinton lied about his relationship with Monica S. Lewinsky, and he allowed his family, cabinet and staff to repeat his lies for seven months while he remained silent. While such behavior may not be actionable for an ordinary citizen, the President should be held to a different standard, regardless of whether his actions constitute high crimes and misdemeanors. (1998, p. A30)

All of these commentaries demonstrate the mixed reaction Clinton's discourse received.

In conclusion, the Prayer Breakfast speech was much more appropriate than the address to the nation. It included the focus on mortification and subsequent corrective action that should have been most prominent from the time he admitted lying.

CONCLUSION

This chapter revealed two distinctly different rhetorical phases in President Clinton's scandal involving Monica Lewinsky. In the first phase, Clinton relied primarily on denial, bolstering, and transcendence. His support as gauged by public opinion polls remained high throughout this phase.

However, as more leaks and physical evidence emerged, he was forced to revise his strategies.

In the second phase, Clinton initially relied mainly on transcendence and attack accuser, but eventually adopted a reliance on mortification and corrective action. His ratings for job performance stayed high while public opinion of Clinton as a person plummeted. His use of transcendence continued to be effective at this time. Indeed, the criteria for enhancing transcendence offered by Benoit and Wells (1998) was met again. As admitted previously, there is no polling data that says the public thought Clinton was distracted by the allegations. However, only the most naive person would dismiss Clinton's media scrutiny as something that did not require his attention. The polling data did show plainly that the public thought the charge was less important than other matters. Additionally, Clinton had won re-election to a second term just barely a year previous to the scandal. One could reasonably argue that the public thought Clinton could affect policy on the issues which were allegedly being neglected.

Moreover, the public did favor some sort of disciplinary action, but not impeachment. The temptation is strong to speculate about how the situation would have differed if Clinton had been truthful from the start. The public appears to have been willing to forgive Clinton to a great extent, even shunning impeachment after he boldly lied publicly and under oath about the matter. Still, Clinton could have spared himself (and the country) much of the aggravation surrounding these incidents if he would have told the truth from the start.

Recall that Benoit, Gullifor and Panici (1991) found that Reagan admitted to wrongdoing only after proof of the misdeed was presented by the Tower Commission. They found that his eventual admission of wrongdoing helped his image repair, but not as much as mortification from the beginning would have repaired it. Likewise, Benoit (1982) found that Nixon admitted wrongdoing only after his guilt was proven, at a time much too late to repair the damage to his presidency.

While Clinton's image restoration strategies were mostly successful, they can be condemned as dishonest. Moreover, quite arguably, he would not have faced the crisis of impeachment if he had opted to tell the truth to the American people and to officers of the court. His lies were a terrible lapse in judgment. As such, his discourse in the Lewinsky matter can be evaluated as generally good, knowing that, like Reagan and Nixon, he could have been yet more effective.

Chapter Eight

The Surrogates: Adultery, Files, and the Travel Office

This chapter will be somewhat different from the previous applications. Three different sets of discourse from three different surrogate defenders of Bill Clinton will be examined: (1) Hillary Clinton's January 27, 1998, appearance on NBC's *Today* show to defend her husband from allegations that he had an illicit affair with Monica Lewinsky; (2) White House Counsel Jack Quinn's and Representative Tom Lantos' June 19, 1996, appearance on CNN's *Larry King Live* program to defend the president from allegations that he had improperly used FBI files for political gain; and (3) White House Chief of Staff Mack McLarty's July 2, 1993, press briefing defending Clinton against accusations of maligning White House Travel Office career employees in order to justify firing and replacing them with political allies.

These texts were chosen because of their unique, situational contexts for defending the president. Hillary Clinton acted as a very personal surrogate defending her husband from very personal charges. The Quinn/Lantos tandem provided an example of combining legalistic and political defense. Finally, as Chief of Staff, Mack McLarty was Clinton's closest advisor with unlimited access to the president himself, and was also a good friend of Clinton's since early childhood.

In each of three major sections in this chapter, the allegations against Clinton will be described, followed by an analysis of the image repair strategies employed. Then, an evaluation will be offered using internal and external data.

HILLARY RODHAM CLINTON AND THE LEWINSKY MATTER

The Persuasive Attack

On January 21, 1998, all of the major news outlets reported that Special Counsel Kenneth Starr was investigating allegations that President Clinton had engaged in a sexual relationship with former White House intern Monica Lewinsky and then encouraged her to deny the relationship under oath. These charges, damaging in themselves, were compounded by the fact that Clinton had (according to leaked Clinton testimony in the Paula Jones sexual harassment case) denied such a relationship with Lewinsky under oath (Froomkin, 1998b). This raised very serious questions regarding possible impeachment proceedings. Legal analyst Stuart Taylor (1998) opined: "If Starr can show that Clinton had sexual relations with Monica Lewinsky and tried to get her to make false denials under oath, then Clinton would be in jeopardy of possible impeachment, eventual criminal prosecution or both" (p. 48). Moreover, if found to be true, the president's credibility as someone whom Americans could take at his word was clearly threatened.

In summary, the charges were four-fold: (1) he had an illicit sexual relationship with a White House intern, (2) he lied about the relationship while under oath, (3) he urged the intern to lie about the relationship under oath, and (4) he obstructed the investigation into this matter.

The Persuasive Defense

Analysis of Hillary Clinton's discourse on behalf of her husband revealed that she used primarily attack accuser and denial, with relatively minor use of bolstering and defeasibility. The strategies will be taken up in that order.

Attack Accuser

Mrs. Clinton relied heavily on the attack accuser strategy. Most of the attacks were directed against Clinton's most vociferous political opponents, rarely naming individual accusers. For instance, she derided the whole accusatory environment: "We're right in the middle of a rather vigorous feeding frenzy right now. People are saying all kinds of things, putting out rumor and innuendo" (H. Clinton, 1998). This statement served to attack those who were creating this environment of rumor and innuendo. Moreover, she referred generically to past allegations: "Bill and I have been accused of everything, including murder, by some of the very same people who are behind these allegations. So from my perspective, this is part of the continuing political campaign against my husband" (H. Clinton, 1998). If the accusers were not credible and politically motivated, then the charges against Clinton should have been deemed less credible.

She continued the general attack against would-be political accusers: "I'm very concerned about the tactics that are being used and the kind of intense political agenda at work here" (H. Clinton, 1998). She also attacked those who would use the justice system to achieve political ends: "It's just a very unfortunate turn of events that we are using the criminal justice system to try to achieve political ends in this country" (H. Clinton, 1998). In both of these instances the attack was implicit. Using the courts to achieve what could not be achieved in the electoral process was improper and vindictive.

Finally, she made her now infamous remark about the nature of the allegedly concerted forces she claimed were aligned against her husband:

> This is the great story here, for anybody willing to find it and write about it and explain it, is this vast right-wing conspiracy that has been conspiring against my husband since the day he announced for president. (H. Clinton, 1998)

In short, Mrs. Clinton attacked accusers as part of an unnamed conspiracy designed to politically destroy the president. If the public could be convinced that the charges were part of some conspiracy, then the allegations might be discredited.

While she reserved most of her ire for generic others, she also mentioned a few names of people who had been particularly evil. Consider the following attack on televangelist Jerry Falwell:

> Having seen so many of these accusations come and go, having seen people profit, you know, like Jerry Falwell, with videos, accusing my husband of committing murder, of drug running, seeing some of the things that are written and said about him, my attitude is, you know, we've been there before, we have seen this before, and I am just going to wait patiently until the truth comes out. (H. Clinton, 1998)

Here, the First Lady attacked Jerry Falwell directly (and others she associated with him) as someone who had made an industry of leveling reckless charges against the president.

Mrs. Clinton also attacked Special Counsel Starr for his alleged motivations:

We get a politically motivated prosecutor who is allied with the right-wing opponents of my husband, who has literally spent four years looking at . . . every telephone call we've made, every check we've ever written, scratching for dirt, intimidating witnesses, doing everything possible to try to make some accusation against my husband. (H. Clinton, 1998)

This clearly served to associate Starr with "right-wing" activists who sought to harm Clinton politically. The statement helped Clinton by impugning the accuser's motives.

She took aim at Starr again, attempting to portray him as part of the "vast right-wing conspiracy" she referred to earlier: "It's not just one person [Starr]. It's an entire operation" (H. Clinton, 1998). Clearly, these statements intended to malign Starr as a politically motivated extremist.

Mrs. Clinton included the three-judge panel that allowed Starr to expand his investigation into the Lewinsky matter among the right-wingers: The panel is "the same three-judge panel that removed Robert Fiske and appointed him [Starr]. The same three-judge panel that is headed by someone who is appointed by Jesse Helms and Lauch Faircloth" (H. Clinton, 1998). In this instance, she leveled ad hominem attacks on the three judges. Her implicit argument was that the panel of judges was not credible because the head was appointed by two arch-conservatives. As such, their decision to expand the investigation should be considered politically motivated as well, potentially discrediting the allegations again.

The above examples illustrate the First Lady's use of attacking accusers. She attacked both an unnamed group of Clinton's political opponents as well as specific Clinton adversaries.

Denial

Mrs. Clinton made two types of denials: (1) that the President had a sexual relationship with Monica Lewinsky; and (2) that Vernon Jordan acted on the president's behalf to silence Lewinsky. Some examples are taken up in that order.

When host Matt Lauer asked if the president's denial of a sexual relationship was true, she replied, "That's right" (H. Clinton, 1998). This served as a simple, brief denial.

Other denials of the relationship centered around Bill Clinton's generous nature, which might explain any hypothetical gifts or special treatment (potentially indicative of an affair) he may have given Lewinsky:

Anyone who knows my husband knows that he is an extremely generous person to people he knows, to strangers, to anyone who is around
him. And I think that, you know, his behavior, his treatment of people
will certainly explain all of this. (H. Clinton, 1998)

Here, she offered an implicit denial of the affair by asserting that giving
gifts to an intern would not be unusual, and thus, not indicative of a sexual
relationship. She continued with this argument: "If you know my husband,
you know that he is somebody who will, you know, say 'Matt, how would
you like this?' I mean, I've seen him take his tie off and hand it to somebody, you know" (H. Clinton, 1998). Asked by Lauer whether such behavior would be typical for Clinton when dealing with an intern, she reiterated:

Dealing with anybody, Matt. I mean, seriously, I have—I've known
my husband for more than 25 years, and we've been married for 22
years, and the one thing I always kid him about is that he never meets a
stranger. He is kind, he is friendly, he tries to help people who need
help, who ask for help. (H. Clinton, 1998)

This statement clearly supported the contention that giving gifts to a
low-level White House operative could easily be explained outside of a sexual context.

These last three examples of denial require some explanation. Clearly,
the statements each bolstered Clinton by referring to his generosity and
helpful character in general. However, I would argue that these bolstering
statements served to deny. Mrs. Clinton's intent behind the statements was
to demonstrate how the president could be genuinely interested in a lowly
intern's career. Establishing his helpfulness was necessary to make the denial plausible. So, the statements did contain elements of bolstering, but
they functioned to deny wrongdoing.

She also denied implicitly a sexual relationship when Lauer asked if the
whole revelation had been a surprise to her: "And to my husband. I mean,
you know, he woke me up Wednesday morning and said 'You're not going
to believe this but . . . ' and I said 'What is this?' And so, yeah, it came as a
very big surprise" (H. Clinton, 1998). In other words, if Bill Clinton had no
idea such a revelation was even thinkable, then there must not have been a
sexual relationship. After all, he had not known about it.

Mrs. Clinton also denied Vernon Jordan had acted to silence Lewinsky
on the president's behalf:

I just can't describe to you how outgoing and friendly Vernon Jordan is. I mean, when he stood up and said what I believe to be the absolute truth, that he has helped literally hundreds of people, and it doesn't matter who they are. And if he were asked to help somebody, he would help that person. I've seen him do it countless times, so I guess I know the people involved. I know them personally. I know them well. I've known Vernon longer than I've known my husband. (H. Clinton, 1998)

Again, just as she did with her husband, she employed bolstering in the service of denial. Since Vernon Jordan had purportedly helped so many people, without regard to their relative importance, his efforts on behalf of Lewinsky in finding employment could not be considered an attempt to quiet her concerning any relationship with Clinton. Thus, she denied that Vernon Jordan had attempted to silence Lewinsky.

Defeasibility

Her one instance of defeasibility addressed the Clintons' overall ability to deal with the allegations in detail: "There's nothing we can do to fight this firestorm of allegations that are out there" (H. Clinton, 1998). This statement served to portray themselves as subject to a flood of charges and unable to respond to the flurry of specific questions.

Bolstering

The bolstering utterance came toward the end of the program segment, and contained a litany of Clinton's achievements: "I think the country is better off because my husband has been president. I think the economy, the crime rate, a lot of the social problems were finally addressed with a smart strategy, and we've seen the results" (H. Clinton, 1998). In short, she claimed Clinton's presidency had been successful. Such an augmentation could surely allay at least some damage brought on by the allegations.

Evaluation

The First Lady's discourse can be evaluated by two criteria: internal consistency and plausibility and external corroboration (public opinion polls and *New York Times* commentary). These criteria will be considered in that order.

By rhetorical standards, Hillary Clinton's discourse was effective in some instances and ineffective in others. Her use of attack was largely effective, associating the accusers with would-be political extremists. By claiming that the accusers had political motivations, the charges could be dismissed as mere partisan foolery.

However, her ad hominem attack on Senators Helms and Faircloth was ill-advised. Contrary to the First Lady's assertion, federal judges are not appointed by senators. Judges are appointed by the executive branch of government. Senators do vote to either confirm or reject appointments. They may also wield unofficial influence over appointments made by presidents of their own party through senatorial privilege (Richard Hardy, personal communication, 1998). But, by no means did Helms or Faircloth appoint any judges. Of course, one could argue that the attack was effective, despite its disingenuousness, because it impugned the panel that warranted the investigation's expansion. If the majority of her audience believed Hillary's assertion that the senators appointed a biased judge, then the charges against Clinton might be discredited to some extent. Still, as an accomplished attorney, Mrs. Clinton surely knew that what she was saying was untrue. Moreover, anyone with an elementary understanding of American civics would know she was lying.

Her use of denial and her descriptions of the president and Vernon Jordan as omni-benevolent were both necessary and effective. The only way she could have explained such benevolence toward Lewinsky would have been as part of their normal, characteristic generosity toward those needing help. Her explanations to Lauer made the efforts of these men plausible, providing some degree of doubt about the allegations.

While her use of defeasibility and bolstering was very minimal, it complemented the attacks and denials appropriately. On balance, Hillary Clinton's discourse could be described as generally effective but not uniformly good.

Polling Data

Polling data indicates that Mrs. Clinton's discourse had a mixed reception. A plurality of those polled (40 percent) thought Clinton had an affair with Lewinsky, compared with 21 percent who thought he had not. However, at the same time, only 26 percent thought he had encouraged her to lie under oath, while a greater number (37 percent) thought he had not, and 33 percent reporting they did not have enough information (Public Opinion Online, 1998a). As such, Mrs. Clinton's denial that her husband had an illicit relationship with Lewinsky was not wholly effective. However, she contributed to the public's doubt over whether the president encouraged Lewinsky to lie.

Commentary

Commentary in the *New York Times* was much more critical. Columnist Maureen Dowd (1998b) questioned Hillary's sincerity:

> Hillary Clinton knows her husband is a hound dog. She knew it before she married him. But they have their deal. He supported her when she messed up on Whitewater and health care. So if the Presidency hinges on "he said, she said," the First Lady won't hesitate to supervise the vivisection of the former intern. (p. A25)

Dowd went on to characterize the First Lady's attitude toward her husband's alleged infidelities:

> The feminist icon in the White House doesn't flinch at smearing these women, even when she suspects they're telling the truth, because she feels they're instruments of a conspiracy. It may turn out that there are right-wing troublemakers involved here, but when Mrs. Clinton uses apocalyptic language, she's just changing the subject. (p. A25)

So, Ms. Dowd did not find Mrs. Clinton's testimony compelling.

Columnist Bob Herbert (1998b) continued with the feminism theme: "Feminists, like other staunch Clinton supporters, are trying to buy time, hoping that the improbable turns out to be true, and rooting this time for the man against the woman" (p. A23). By describing the denials as "improbable," he hinted at his skepticism toward the explanations given.

Frank Rich (1998c) continued the litany of criticism against the image repair discourse:

> Is it possible that a vast left-wing conspiracy has been plotting against Kenneth Starr and anyone else who would bring the President down? The brilliant leader of this conspiracy would be Hillary Clinton, who ingeniously deflected suspicion this week with her "Today" show appearance [claim] that a right-wing conspiracy had installed a heat-seeking Monica in the White House. (p. A15)

Clearly, Rich leveled sarcasm against Mrs. Clinton's claim of a "vast right-wing conspiracy." Sarcasm directed at one's statements usually indicates contempt for what was said. As such, one could conclude that Rich did not agree with Hillary's discourse.

Only Lawrence H. Pelofsky's (1998) letter to the editor provided sympathy for the Clintons, in the form of an attack on Kenneth Starr: "I find the desire of Kenneth Starr, the independent counsel, to gather the facts quickly and get at the truth of Monica S. Lewinsky's tape-recorded allegations to strain credulity" (p. A22). Here, Pelofsky reflected Hillary's position that Starr's investigation was not about fact gathering, but rather, a partisan inquisition.

Summary

Chapter Seven demonstrated that in the long-term, the public did not believe Bill Clinton's denials of an illicit relationship. However, early in the scandal, during the week following Hillary's appearance on the *Today* show, the public appeared divided over the matter. A plurality thought Clinton had the affair with Lewinsky. By this measure, one could say that Hillary's denials were ineffective. However, this plurality was smaller than the majorities that would emerge later. As such, one could argue that Mrs. Clinton's discourse had a mixed effectiveness.

THE FBI FILES

The Persuasive Attack

On June 19, 1996, Republicans Representative Bill Clinger and Senator Orrin Hatch appeared on CNN's *Larry King Live* program to assert that the Clinton administration had unlawfully obtained hundreds of confidential FBI files of numerous Republicans. The two charged that (1) the files were illicitly obtained for political purposes, and (2) that Clinton was late in responding to the allegations. If these could have been proven, the administration would have faced a devastating loss of credibility and possibly legal repercussions. Republican Steve Forbes (1996) charged that the incident should be considered an impeachable offense:

> The White House's obtaining hundreds of FBI files on Republicans with previous White House clearance is an egregious, outrageous abuse of power. . . . Severe punishments are in order. A vibrant democracy should not tolerate this kind of behavior. (p. 23)

If the public came to believe that Clinton had used the power of his office to debilitate his political foes, he may have risked public support. Since he was facing reelection in a few short months, image repair in response to these allegations was necessary.

The Persuasive Defense

Later in the same program, White House Counsel Jack Quinn and Democratic Representative Tom Lantos appeared to defend the administration from the accusations. The two used nine of the fourteen restoration strategies: attack accuser, denial, minimization, bolstering, accident, corrective action, transcendence, defeasibility, and shift blame. However, the analysis revealed that they relied mostly on attack accuser, denial, and minimization. The strategies will be discussed in order of prominence in the discourse.

Attack Accuser

Quinn and Lantos used attacks to defend Clinton on several occasions. For instance, Lantos chided the Republicans for being hypocritical:

> Now some of my Republican colleagues will not be satisfied until the President commits hari-kari and that is not part of the American political culture. The degree of sanctimoniousness and hypocrisy which oozes from some of my colleagues in these hearings is beyond belief. (Lantos, 1996)

Lantos accused Republicans of being sanctimonious and hypocritical, two qualities a politician would certainly want to avoid. If the Clinton's detractors could be described in such a way, then their accusations could be discredited to some extent.

Quinn also attacked Republican attitudes toward the investigation in general:

> We have learned that when the White House itself, or the Counsel's office in the White House conducts an investigation, it is apt, in these particular political times, to lead only to charges by the Republican opposition that the investigation of the matter is itself somehow flawed. (Quinn, 1996)

In short, Quinn argued that the Republicans would unnecessarily scrutinize any effort the administration made to address the issue. By portraying the accusers as unreasonable, the charges against Clinton could be mitigated.

Denial

Quinn and Lantos made two basic denials: (1) the files had not been procured for political purposes, and (2) Clinton was not delinquent in providing an explanation of the matter. Quinn made perhaps the most important denial when he asserted that the files had not been retrieved as part of an "enemies" list: "So that requests were made for the FBI reports, not just of a former Chief of Staff, or other well-recognized people like that, but of groundskeepers and people who worked on the telephones and other people" (Quinn, 1996). In short, Quinn said there was no systematic collection of files of notable Republicans, and therefore, a deliberate composition of an "enemies" list had never occurred. This denial could deflect the charge that Clinton had an improper political "enemies list."

When guest-host Wolf Blitzer asked why it took three and a half years for Clinton to make a substantial response to the file fiasco, Lantos denied Clinton was late in making amends: "Well, it's not too late because it emerged now" (Lantos, 1996). In other words, Lantos denied that Clinton took action too late in his term. If he could succeed in denying Clinton had delayed, then the public might not perceive Clinton as trying to be evasive.

Minimization

Minimization was also used on two occasions. For instance, when asked why he had not turned over the 2,000 documents that Republicans had been asking for, Quinn shot back, "Well, first of all, it's 2,000 pages, not 2,000 documents" (Quinn, 1996). Lantos provided another example, describing what he thought was the minor nature of the offense: "The only evidence we have so far is that two relatively low-level operatives did some incredibly stupid things" (Lantos, 1996). Here, the minimization is manifest in Lantos' attempt to show that relatively minor players in the administration had performed the misdeed in question. As such, the incident was not as insidious as it would have been if key players in the administration had been the offenders. One might argue that Lantos was shifting blame away from Clinton. That is not the focus of his message. Lantos' primary argument here was that the file incident was minor in nature. Both of these instances attempted to repair Clinton's image by downplaying the seriousness of the charges.

Bolstering

The bolstering strategy was employed in order to play up Clinton's strengths in spite of the files incident. For example, Quinn spoke on behalf of the administration: "We have made clear that we are perfectly willing to try to accommodate the Congress' legitimate interest in getting information that it genuinely needs" (Quinn, 1996). This statement enhanced the administration's image as cooperative.

Accident

Accident was used to demonstrate that the administration acknowledged wrongdoing had occurred. Quinn noted the contrition: "Congressman Lantos and everyone else has acknowledged this, as has the White House, that not only did something most unfortunate, perhaps stupid, happen here, but that it was a very serious mistake, it was very, very serious" (Quinn, 1996). Quinn acknowledged that the president considered the action a mistake. By claiming the action was an accident, Clinton's image could be repaired since the deed was not done purposefully. One could also note that the statement also served to bolster Clinton, underscoring the seriousness with which Clinton considered the transgression.

Corrective Action

Having admitted wrongdoing, it is not surprising that corrective action was offered as well. Quinn assured, "At the President's direction, we have now put in place absolutely unprecedented and rigorous procedures which will guarantee that this never happens again" (Quinn 1996). So, Quinn promised not only corrective action, but substantial actions beyond any previous attempts at correction.

Transcendence

Quinn punctuated his description of the corrective system set in place with an argument for transcendence: "Now we have to move on with real issues facing the American people" (Quinn, 1996). This statement promoted the notion that the indiscretion at hand was not relevant to "the American people," and that there was more important business at hand.

Defeasibility

Quinn used defeasibility to defend the administration from charges that they were slow to produce requested documents: "Let me make clear to you that we're faced right now with no fewer than about a half a dozen requests from various Congressional committees" (Quinn, 1996). Clearly, Quinn argued that they were having trouble physically complying with the requests because there were so many requests for information.

Shift Blame

Finally, Quinn shifted the blame for hiring Craig Livingstone (who procured the FBI files) away from the president: "Look, it's very easy to look back and second guess a hire that somebody else made" (Quinn, 1996). In other words, the president should not be judged for the actions of another (whoever hired Livingstone).

In summary, Quinn and Lantos relied most heavily on attack accuser, denial, and minimization. However, they also engaged to a lesser degree in bolstering, accident, corrective action, transcendence, defeasibility, and shift the blame.

Evaluation

Quinn and Lantos' discourse on behalf of Clinton can be judged by two criteria: internal consistency and plausibility and external corroboration. The criteria will be treated in that order.

Rhetorically, Quinn and Lantos made poor choices. Attacking the accusers (Republicans) was appropriate to the extent that Quinn and Lantos took issue with the nature of the investigations and Republican reluctance to let the issue die. However, their reliance on attack accuser in this context might be questioned because they admitted wrongdoing by the administration. This does not mean that using attack accuser and mortification ought to be mutually exclusive. However, one might have expected more use of mortification and corrective action because of the seriousness of the charges. They did a fine job of describing the deed as the innocuous antics of a low-level bureaucrat. However, such widespread violations of privacy are serious, regardless of one's intent for the act or one's bureaucratic stature. Apologies and assurances of prevention were in order.

Even though they could not deny wrongdoing, Quinn and Lantos used denial insofar as they denied that the files were part of some "enemies" list and that Clinton had ordered the files. In fact, one could argue that such a denial was absolutely necessary in order to maintain the perception of a responsible presidency. Even if Clinton had not known about the procurement, the compilation of secret information about political rivals by anyone in the White House would have been extremely damaging. The denials here were necessary, but not sufficient, for restoring President Clinton's reputation.

Minimization was also used efficiently to downplay the severity of the offense. By describing the alleged perpetrators as "lower" level employees, one could argue that the deed was not as serious as if it had been carried out by someone in the president's cabinet.

The other strategies, though employed less frequently, were also well advised. In particular, accident was appropriate because the files were illegally obtained. Official recognition that the misdeed took place could tend to increase the president's perception as someone who told the truth. Denying something that had observably taken place would have been foolish. Furthermore, the use of corrective action was appropriate. Describing to one's audience how the situation which made the mistakes possible could be fixed would surely provide some comfort to those who were offended by the misdeed.

Polling Data

The public polling data universally indicate that the public did not believe Clinton or his surrogates regarding "Filegate." Fully 60 percent of those polled thought the White House was trying to hide something (Public Opinion Online, 1996a). Fifty-six percent thought the files incident represented an intentional abuse of power (Public Opinion Online, 1996b). Furthermore, 50 percent of those polled thought the misdeed was done with Clinton's knowledge, with only 36 percent saying they thought Clinton had no knowledge of the abuse (Public Opinion Online, 1996b).

Commentary

Commentary from the *New York Times* also indicates that the image repair following the files scandal may not have been adequate to restore trust in Clinton's presidency (although not enough to warrant impeachment at that time). Maureen Dowd (1996) asked the rhetorical question of why the Clintons had surrounded themselves with "sleazeballs":

The answer—despite the President's tut-tutting at the FBI dirt on the White House rug—may well be that the Clintons are in need of sleazeball services. This is a White House that prizes loyalty over maturity, politics over government, polling over principles, a place where righteousness is measured by rapid response. (p. E13)

Here, Dowd indicated that she had not accepted the claim that the FBI files incident was out of the ordinary for an administration that was so apparently corrupt.

Columnist William Safire (1996) also described the files fiasco as typical for the Clintons:

Vince Foster, afflicted with the festering Whitewater files, was the first to crack, a suicide. The too-loyal [Bernard] Nussbaum, blocking the FBI from the dead man's office files on Whitewater, was soon cut adrift by his clients. William Kennedy, who tried to cover up a patronage grab by using the FBI to besmear innocent travel office staffers, quit under a cloud. His role as supervisor of the former bouncer Livingstone in raping the privacy of some 500 Americans is just being exposed. (p. A15)

Clearly, Safire did not believe that the procurement of files was without political purpose.

While Dowd and Safire were more direct in their criticism, Russell Baker (1996) used sarcasm to describe his reaction:

Is President Clinton unscrupulous enough to use the FBI files against Republicans? Come, come, we must not even think such thoughts about a President just because FBI files have come into the possession of Presidential assistants who may be slightly unscrupulous, at least when a re-election campaign is in progress. (p. A21)

One should interpret the above as sarcasm, truly intended to state plainly that Clinton wanted the FBI files for political purposes. Clearly, the commentary about Clinton following Quinn and Lantos' joint *apologia* session was critical, even though I would maintain they did a respectable job.

Summary

In summary, Quinn and Lantos relied on attack accuser, denial, and minimization when defending Clinton in the wake of the FBI files scandal. Their discourse was ineffective. Commentary and public polling data indicate that the issue continued to harm Clinton's image. The public believed Clinton knew about the file procurement and had engaged in an intentional abuse of power. Luckily for Clinton, there was no evidence that the files had actually been used.

THE WHITE HOUSE TRAVEL OFFICE

The Persuasive Attack

On May 21, 1993, the White House announced that the accounting firm of Peter Marwick had conducted an audit of the White House Travel Office and found wasteful practices in procuring travel for the administration and the White House press pool. Concurrent with the audit, the administration asked the Justice Department to investigate any wrongdoing at the office headed by a career employee named Billy Dale. In the course of Justice's investigation, Dale and others were maligned, fired, and accused of financial misdeeds in the office even though their actions had been standard practice for years. Moreover, five of those seven employees had no financial decision-making powers in the office. Senators Robert Dole of Kansas and Kit Bond of Missouri included payment of the staff's legal fees in a Department of Transportation bill. Devroy (1993) explained that Dole and Bond

> introduced the amendment to cover the legal fees for the five rein-
> stated workers because they were the "true, real-life victims" of the
> debacle. They "woke up one May morning only to hear their good rep-
> utations smeared on national television by an incompetent White
> House staff. They were accused of "gross mismanagement" and sub-
> jected to an FBI investigation. (p. A21)

When the press found out that Clinton planned to replace the staff with Arkansas cronies recommended by Clinton friend Harry Thomason, a pa-tronage scandal appeared to be materializing. The editorial page summa-rized these charges:

> One of the aides who wanted and got the job of running the reconsti-
> tuted travel office was a distant presidential cousin. One of the people
> inquiring about the travel office business was a presidential friend
> with a White House pass and the apparent run of the White House,
> who turned out himself to have an interest in a travel company. (The
> travel office, 1993, p. C6)

Even worse, the White House's own report on the matter indicated three more disturbing facts: (1) First Lady Hillary Rodham Clinton made inqui-ries about the progress of taking over the office; (2) the official who fired the staffers suggested that the White House press secretary describe the fir-ings as part of Vice President Gore's effort to "reinvent government"; and (3) senior White House aids contacted the FBI to "clarify" one of its press releases to corroborate a White House press release on the matter (*Wash-ington Post*, p. C6).

Writing for the conservative *American Spectator*, investigative reporter David Brock (1994) described the whole process:

> It is the full story of Travelgate. The plan to replace the White House
> travel office with a hand-picked travel agency, World Wide Travel of
> Little Rock, was hatched shortly after the 1992 election. But it was
> rooted in long-standing political and business relationships in Arkan-
> sas. . . . A second look at the scandal reveals an array of hidden agen-
> das and payback schemes implicating the president. (p. 30)

Clearly, Clinton faced an image crisis since he (1) appeared to be not only vicious in his destruction of Dale's reputation, but also (2) corrupt in hiring political friends for career, professional positions.

The Persuasive Defense

On July 2, 1993, White House Chief of Staff Mack McLarty addressed the White House press corps in the Briefing Room to respond to the allegations of corruption and maliciousness. McLarty primarily used mortification and corrective action. He also used bolstering, shift blame, and good intentions, but to a much lesser degree. The strategies will be discussed in that order.

Mortification

McLarty used mortification most frequently. The first instance set the tone for the rest of his speech: "This report details that mistakes were made and identifies some ill-advised actions" (McLarty, 1993). He conceded that the actions were mistakes and ill-advised. After that statement, he proceeded to apologize for three basic misdeeds: implementing changes in the Travel Office in an unorthodox fashion, mistreating the Travel Office employees, and letting Harry Thomason make administrative recommendations.

McLarty recognized that the process for change was flawed: "To our regret, we erred in implementing these needed changes. From a management standpoint, in other words, we did the right thing [reformed the Travel Office] but we clearly did it in the wrong way" (McLarty, 1993). Here, he recognized that the changes were implemented improperly, though he did not express regret for the changes themselves.

Another example demonstrated mortification for mistreatment of the employees: "This action clearly should have been handled in a more sensitive manner, in retrospect" (McLarty, 1993). Clearly, this statement admitted wrongdoing toward the career employees.

Finally, an example of mortification over Harry Thomason's role in the fiasco was offered:

The report addresses Harry Thomason's involvement in this matter also. Though it may have been appropriate for Mr. Thomason to suggest potential areas for improvement and savings, his persistence led to the perception that he was intervening. The White House Office of Management and Administration and the Chief of Staff's Office should have thanked Mr. Thomason for his information, looked into the matter seriously, but certainly more deliberately and carefully. (McLarty, 1993)

This statement recognized that Mr. Thomason (a friend of the Clintons, but not a staffer) should not have been so involved with the decision to fire the Travel Office staff. The above examples demonstrate McLarty's use of mortification.

Corrective Action

Of course, where one admits wrongdoing, one might also offer plans to prevent such recurrences. McLarty offered several instances of corrective action, including a general statement of intentions to improve the situation: "The review ascertained what happened in the Travel Office matter, and as a result, we are implementing improvements in procedures" (McLarty, 1993). This statement indicated a responsive attitude and willingness to take corrective action.

McLarty described a specific act affecting the employees: "At my direction, action was taken later to extend indefinitely the paid administrative leave of the five employees who had no financial authority" (McLarty, 1993). In other words, the innocent employees who had been harmed were being paid while the matter was being investigated further.

McLarty listed further corrective action:

The mistakes call for some corrective actions, and these are also outlined in the report. They include: The Counsel to the President has issued a revised guidance to all White House personnel clarifying that initial White House contacts concerning ongoing FBI investigations or criminal activity will occur only between the Counsel's Office and the Attorney General, Deputy Attorney General, or Associate Attorney General. (McLarty, 1993)

This statement offered an explanation of how future contacts between the administration and the FBI would occur. McLarty went on to list other actions:

Secondly, the Counsel to the President has issued a revised guidance to all White House personnel clarifying that it is never appropriate to contact the IRS to initiate an audit. Thirdly, the White House Press Office will not disclose ongoing investigations except in extraordinary circumstances and only with the approval of the White House Counsel and Chief of Staff or Deputy Chief of Staff. The Director of Communications has issued guidance to all White House Communications

Department personnel which clarifies the procedures for contacts between the FBI Public Affairs Office and the White House Press Office. (McLarty, 1993)

In short, on this occasion McLarty offered a litany of actions to be taken in recourse.

All of the above examples demonstrate his use of corrective action. While McLarty used mostly mortification and corrective action, he used other strategies minimally as well. Those examples are provided in the following sections.

Bolstering

McLarty also bolstered the administration in order to mitigate any wrongdoing. For instance, he discussed the benefits of the changes they had implemented: The Travel Office's previous ineffectiveness "is established not only by this review, but is also confirmed with the savings we already achieved from different management practices and competitive bidding" (McLarty, 1993). This statement served to bolster the administration's image as efficient reformers.

Shift Blame

McLarty shifted the blame for the unnecessary FBI investigation to the FBI itself: "I would note that the FBI, with the concurrence of Justice Department officials, determined on its own to commence an investigation" (McLarty, 1993). In other words, the FBI became involved at its own behest, not at the prodding of the White House. The administration should not be blamed for the FBI's involvement.

Good Intentions

McLarty explained the improper meeting between the FBI and the White House: "Those attending the meeting were acting in good faith" (McLarty, 1993). In other words, the meeting was not intended to harm innocent people, but only to provide good, efficient government.

In summary, McLarty relied heavily on mortification and corrective action. Bolstering, shift blame, good intentions, and denial were also used, though much less frequently.

Evaluation

This discourse can be evaluated by two criteria: internal consistency and plausibility and external corroboration. (Note that there were no *New York*

Times commentaries about this subject for the week following the press conference, and as such, polling data served as external corroboration.) The criteria will be taken up in that order.

McLarty's use of mortification and corrective action was well-advised. After all, the allegations that the White House had prompted the Travel Office firings was demonstrably true. As such, denial of the misdeed would invariably have hurt Clinton's credibility further (though McLarty did deny the smaller detail of contacting the IRS). Moreover, it is fitting that substantial mortification be accompanied by much detailing of corrective action. Mortification and corrective action form an expected apologetic couplet in this sense. Moreover, it was also proper for McLarty to insulate the president from the admissions of wrongdoing by speaking generically of the offenders as various White House staffers.

McLarty should have limited his discourse to those strategies. He also shifted blame to the FBI and argued for good intentions. Shifting the blame when one has clearly engaged in misbehavior makes one appear unrepentant. Moreover, trying to convince an audience of the good intentions of an act when the act was quite publicly self-interested is difficult. For the same reason, bolstering the White House's progress in the Travel Office was unwarranted.

Polling Data

By rhetorical standards, McLarty's discourse was weak. Moreover, polling data in the next election cycle indicates that the public thought that Clinton was guilty of wrongdoing. Forty-nine percent of those polled thought Clinton had lied about his role in the Travel Office firings, while only 32 percent thought he had told the truth. Moreover, 41 percent thought Clinton had done something illegal, compared with the 36 percent who thought he was innocent in the matter (Public Opinion Online, 1996a).

Summary

McLarty's discourse in his press briefing was ineffective. The Travel Office issue continued to tarnish Clinton's image. The public continued to believe that Clinton acted immorally or illegally. However, again, most Americans did not believe the charges were damning.

CONCLUSION

This chapter examined image repair discourse from surrogates in three rhetorical situations. Hillary Clinton's defense of her husband following allegations of his affair with Monica Lewinsky received a mixed reaction. White House Counsel Quinn and Representative Lantos' defense of the president in the wake of "Filegate" failed to erase Clinton's perception as acting immorally in the matter. Finally, Chief of Staff Mack McLarty offered a weak defense of Clinton following the Travel Office firings. Again, the public tended to believe that Clinton had acted both immorally and illegally.

An interesting commonality existed in the three sets of discourse. Each of the rhetors chose to bolster President Clinton, the man for whom they were speaking. This makes sense given that these surrogates were essentially performing public relations duties for the president. A good public relations representative will naturally want the public to know about the client's positive traits. Additionally, a president who bolsters himself may appear immodest or simply opportunistic. The surrogate may be able to provide needed praise in a more credible fashion.

Benoit and Wells (1998) argued that some surrogates may be effective insofar as they appear more objective than the accused. This chapter discovered a limitation on that theory. Hillary, Quinn/Lantos, and McLarty were each perceived as personally or politically tied to Clinton. This may have diminished their perceived objectivity, although it certainly would not make them appear less objective than Clinton.

One might also surmise that the surrogate is uniquely situated to attack the accuser, especially on behalf of someone like the president. The president is expected to maintain a dignified image of the leader who speaks for all Americans. Attacking one's opponents (even political rivals) could make him/her look unpresidential. As such, the surrogates may function to level attacks (though McLarty made no such attacks here).

The denial strategies employed here are notable. Only Hillary denied outright that any wrongdoing had taken place, in this case denying that the president had an affair with Monica Lewinsky and had encouraged her to lie about it under oath. Quinn/Lantos and McLarty also used denial, but not with respect to the primary accusations. For instance, Quinn/Lantos did not deny FBI files had been illegally obtained, but they did deny that they were used politically. Likewise, McLarty did not deny that the Travel Office employees had been unjustly treated, but he did deny that the Travel Office firings were part of a patronage scheme.

One might surmise that the First Lady was a surrogate so closely associated with the president that she would not have been the choice to represent her husband had an admission of wrongdoing been part of the strategy. Indeed, as his wife, she was an able spokeswoman for his denials. It is notable that she was a primary surrogate for the president in the matter of marital infidelity. She may have been perfectly suited for the duty given her direct interest in the matter. Moreover, her appearance may have had an implicit message as well: "Even if he did stray, he's my husband and I'm completely behind him." Let me be clear about this. She *did not* make this statement. However, one could easily predict her unconditional support for her husband, even if she knew he had been unfaithful. Her presence as a trusting wife was personal and powerful in the Lewinsky matter. This power would not be as apparent in a nonmarital context.

On the other hand, Quinn, Lantos, and McLarty were all tied to Clinton in official capacities. As such, they could serve as able surrogates for the president when mortification was necessary.

However, the surrogate as expressor of mortification poses a potential problem. The public, if sufficiently offended by a misdeed, may require that mortification come from the offender, not a surrogate. That situation could place a considerable limitation on the surrogate's usefulness.

Notably, Clinton's meeting of Benoit and Wells' (1998) criteria for enhancing transcendence is difficult to assess in this application. Clearly, the public must have thought the FBI files matter was unimportant compared to policy issues. A majority thought he had broken the law and still did not consider the matter as pressing. There is no data that shows the public thought Clinton was distracted by the issue. However, the fact that Clinton gave no substantial amount of oratory on the matter indicates that he was relatively unconcerned (or at least wanted to be perceived as such by the public). Again, there is no data saying that the public thought Clinton should have addressed any neglected issues, but they certainly gave him a high approval rating. In summary, the criteria for enhancing the transcendence used by Clinton's surrogates appears to have been present. Of course, as discussed, these sets of discourse were lackluster in other ways.

In spite of largely unsuccessful surrogate defenses, these allegations did not substantially hurt Clinton, particularly in the FBI files and Travel Office matter. Indeed, the public believed he had broken the law. However, more importantly, the public never found the wrongdoing serious enough to merit their outrage.

Chapter Nine

Conclusion

In this chapter, the results of the applications will be integrated to discuss the theoretical contributions of this study, admit some limitations, and propose areas for future research. It will begin with a review of which strategies were used to what effect in each study. After that, the theoretical implications will be discussed. This will be followed by sections addressing limitations and possibilities for future research.

REVIEW OF STRATEGIES

Chapter Three—To Serve or Not to Serve: Clinton's Draft Record

In Clinton's first brush with major scandal in his 1992 campaign, he relied on the denial and bolstering strategies. He denied doing anything illegal during his period of draft eligibility during the late 1960s. Also, he denied acting opportunistically within the letter of the law in order to evade the draft. He used bolstering to talk about his general patriotism and military leadership of the Arkansas National Guard. He also used defeasibility, transcendence, differentiation, good intentions, minimization, and attack accuser to a lesser extent. See Table 9.1.

His discourse was largely effective in spite of the series of events in 1969 that could lead one to believe that Clinton had no intention of participating in the draft voluntarily. There was no evidence that he broke the letter of the law. Moreover, the charge that he evaded the draft opportunistically was

Table 9.1
Breakdown of Clinton Strategies

Scandal	Accusation	Major Strategy	Minor Strategy
Draft	Violated laws	SD	-
	evaded draft	SD	DE, DI, GI, MN
	lacked credibility/ patriotism	BL	AA
	-	-	TR
Flowers	adultery	SD	BL, AA, DI
	disqualified	TR	-
Marijuana	smoked pot	MN	-
	evasive	SD	-
	wounded candidacy	SD	-
Whitewater	inappropriate influence	SD	SB, CA
	hinder investigation	BL	DI, AA
	improper contact	SD	MO
	conflict of interest	SD	DE, DI, MN
	-	TR	-
Lewinsky	adultery	SD(1), MO(3), CA(3)	MO(2), GI(2), TR(3)
	perjury	-	SD(2), MN(2), DI(3)
	subornation	SD(1)	SD(2)
	obstruction	SD(1)	SD(2)
	-	AA(2), TR(2)	BL(1), TR(1), MO(2), CA(2), BL(3), AA(3)
Surrogates			
Hillary	adultery	SD	-
	subornation	SD	-
	perjury	-	-
	obstruction	-	-
	-	AA, DE, BL	-
Quinn/	abuse power	SD, MN	BL, AC, CA, TR, SB
Lantos	stalling	-	DE
	-	AA	-
McLarty	harm employees	MO, CA	BL, GI, SD, SB
	patronage scheme	MO	-

Abbreviation Key: SD-simple denial, SB-shift blame, DE-defeasibility, AC-accident, GI-good intentions, BL-bolstering, MN-minimization, DI-differentiation, TR-transcendence, AA-attack accuser, CA-corrective action, MO-mortification

(1) denotes first discourse set, (2) denotes second, (3) denotes third

Major strategies are those which are used most frequently. Minor strategies are less dominant.

deflected by his assertions of patriotism. While these strategies did not please everybody, they convinced enough voters in New Hampshire that he was a viable presidential candidate.

Chapter Four—"Pain in My Marriage": Gennifer Flowers and Infidelity

In this chapter dealing with allegations of adultery, Clinton used denial, bolstering, attack accuser, transcendence, and differentiation. He directly denied having an affair with Gennifer Flowers, but was more equivocal with denials of adultery in general. Despite its falsity, this denial was probably effective. Without conclusive evidence of the affair available to his accusers at the time, his denial served the immediate purpose of repairing his image in time for the presidential primary. Moreover, his use of transcendence mitigated the public's concerns about the importance of the allegations.

His other strategies were each appropriate for the given charges. Polling data, commentary, and the election outcomes show that he maintained an image adequate to his short-term electoral goals.

Chapter Five—"But I Didn't Inhale": The Marijuana Controversy

Pressed for information about his use (or nonuse) of illegal drugs, Clinton used minimization when he admitted to smoking marijuana while denying having "inhaled" the substance. Polling data showed that his discourse did more to damage than repair his image. Commentators found the explanation laughable. The "but I didn't inhale" line has since become one of our country's best inside jokes. This instance demonstrated that a direct admission of wrongdoing is more effective than attempts to minimize the misdeed in some disingenuous way.

Fortunately for Clinton, most of those polled said that his discourse had neither a positive nor negative influence. Moreover, the scarcity of commentary found in the *New York Times* indicated that the marijuana issue may not have been altogether disturbing to most people. Many may have come to the conclusion that experimentation with pot in the 1960s was so widespread that it was no longer a disqualifying offense for a presidential candidate. As such, one can surmise that the severity of allegations, not merely their truth/falsity, matters in image repair. This possibility further underscores the judgment that Clinton should have simply admitted to isolated use of marijuana and watched the issue subside.

Chapter Six—Land Ho!: Whitewater

In this chapter, Clinton engaged primarily in bolstering, but also used multiple examples of denial and transcendence. His several instances of bolstering addressed his cooperation. This was an apt strategy because his withholding of requested information certainly may have appeared to be stonewalling.

The discourse had a mixed reaction, but it was ultimately effective. Polling and commentary showed that the public wanted a special prosecutor appointed. However, a majority of Americans still did not consider the matter as pressing or urgent. Moreover, Clinton won reelection by a wide margin, demonstrating again that the severity of allegations is just as important in image restoration as perceived guilt or innocence.

Chapter Seven—That Woman: The Lewinsky Affair

This chapter described two rhetorical phases with three rhetorical strategies used in the Monica Lewinsky matter. In the first phase Clinton relied on denial, but also engaged in bolstering and transcendence. His job approval and personal favorability ratings remained high in this period, indicating his discourse had been effective.

However, in the second phase physical evidence (a semen stain on Lewinsky's dress) was allegedly recovered that would conclude that the president's denial of a sexual relationship had been a lie. Moreover, in his August 17, 1998, grand jury testimony, Clinton admitted to an "inappropriate" relationship. In his address to the nation that evening, he admitted to wrongdoing, but unwisely relied on transcendence and attack accuser. In other words, in what should have been a humbling address he appeared insufficiently contrite. On top of all of this, he persisted in his denial of lying under oath in the Jones deposition, calling that testimony "legally accurate." His personal favorability rating plummeted overnight, though his job performance rating remained high. Prominent members of his own party (including Senators Feinstein, Moynihan, and Lieberman) sharply rebuked him on the Senate floor and other public venues (Polls show job approval, 1998). This was clearly a setback as each of these senators would have a vote in any impending impeachment trial. Moreover, that these critics were political allies made the reaction more damning. Clearly, this portion of Clinton's discourse in the Lewinsky matter was ineffective.

Only during his speech at the September 11, 1998, White House Prayer Breakfast did Clinton engage in the necessary mortification and corrective action. Ultimately, his discourse was effective. One might argue that he could have avoided his eventual humiliation had he admitted to wrongdoing when the charges were first publicized. Had he been more truthful, perhaps his perception as a human being could have been salvaged. However, the polling data showed that the majority of Americans supported his presidency.

His rhetorical success may be properly judged by two potential goals. If Clinton's goal was to avoid damage to his reputation and escape punishment, he failed. In the end, a majority of Americans wanted him punished, either through censure or impeachment. A small minority wanted the issue dropped.

However, if his goal was to remain in office, he succeeded. The 1998 midterm elections resulted in a net Republican loss of seats in the House of Representatives coupled with no increase in Senate seats. This was a major setback for Clinton's Republican accusers since the party not holding the White House at midterm traditionally makes significant congressional gains (Polls show job approval, 1998). One could interpret the results as a rejection of Republican impeachment efforts. Consider that the Republican National Committee, at the direction of Newt Gingrich, ran a last-minute, $10 million ad campaign raising the issue of Clinton's infidelities and lies (Polls show job approval, 1998). The outcome of this election left the Republicans with their original number of fifty-five Senate seats. Sixty-seven Senate votes would be required for an impeachment conviction. Ultimately, Clinton was acquitted.

Chapter 8–The Surrogates: Adultery, Files, and the Travel Office

This chapter revealed that Clinton's surrogates bolstered his image regularly. Also, they attacked his accusers, perhaps performing this function more aggressively than Clinton could (questioning the character of his accusers), or at times when it would be unpresidential for Clinton to do so himself (for instance, verbally attacking an intern who worked in his office might appear brutal). Polling data and commentary found that Hillary Rodham Clinton's denials of her husband's adultery were not believed. This might be due to Bill Clinton's own denials being perceived as carefully worded rather than categorical. Jack Quinn and Tom Lantos' attacks and denials did not help Clinton's image. Decisive majorities thought Clinton was trying to hide something and believed he was engaging in intentional abuse of power. One explanation for this could be the public's wondering *why* the files had been procured if not for the political treachery Quinn and Lantos denied. Perhaps the public also had trouble believing FBI files could be ordered without the president's knowledge. Finally, White House Chief of Staff Mack McLarty engaged in mortification, corrective action, bolstering, shift blame, and good intentions. These rhetorical strategies were designed to insulate the president from appearing corrupt in his dealings with the Travel Office. Yet, the public persisted in its belief that Clinton had engaged in immoral behavior and had knowingly broken the law. It could be possible that because a friend and a distant cousin of Clinton were likely beneficiaries of the White House actions, the denials of patronage and maliciousness were hard to believe.

The above descriptions show that Clinton's image restoration throughout his presidency has been largely effective, but not universally. However, the efforts have been sufficient to sustain his approval ratings and a reelection campaign. As previously mentioned, the public did not find some of the offenses serious enough to merit any real trouble for Clinton. He has managed to avoid removal, although some might not necessarily hail that as a great rhetorical accomplishment.

Table 9.1 illustrates Clinton's rhetorical choices. For example, eleven out of twenty of the major strategies he employed were simple denial. He used this strategy at least once in each scandal. Transcendence was used in three of the five scandals he addressed. It is also notable that he usually relied on one major strategy (predominantly used strategies) per accusation. In contrast, he usually used multiple minor strategies (less frequently used strategies) for a given episode. He used attack accuser at least once in each of the scandals except for his explanation about marijuana use (which was a very small discourse set). This demonstrates that Clinton believed in the rhetorical value of discrediting the people who charged him with wrongdoing. The public opinion polling that shows more people blame Starr than Clinton for the Monica Lewinsky scandal is an obvious example of how these attacks can be successful. Moreover, his attacks were usually a minor strategy. This indicates that he chose not to be perceived as *focused* on the foibles of others. He also used differentiation in each scandal (save for the marijuana issue), exclusively as a minor strategy.

Clinton's surrogates, on the other hand, used attack accuser as a major strategy, excluding McLarty who was giving an expressly apologetic speech. Not surprisingly, they each bolstered Clinton's reputation. In addition, leaving the attacks to the surrogates enabled Clinton to focus on his strongest strategy, transcendence, while still being assured that the credibility of his accusers would be questioned.

THEORETICAL IMPLICATIONS

This section on theoretical implications will address seven major topics: (1) the image repair strategies that are better understood because of this study; (2) the study's contribution to understanding surrogates in image repair discourse; (3) Clinton's image restoration style; (4) the importance of the severity of accusations; (5) the role of triangulation in rhetorical evaluations; (6) the appropriateness of Benoit's (1995a) method for this study; and (7) the distinction between repairing image, avoiding legal punishment, and maintaining power in political image restoration. The topics will be addressed in that order.

Clarification of Strategies

The most important findings about individual strategies in this study address transcendence. Clinton's discourse addressing the various accusations presented in the preceding chapters was largely, if not uniformly, successful. One should note that a common strategic thread ran through all of the discourse: transcendence. This ability to describe charges against him as unimportant in the larger context of America's challenges was the key to his rhetorical success.

Benoit and Wells (1998) studied Whitewater-related image repair and found three criteria that enhance the transcendence strategy when the rhetor claims that the given charges are a distraction from more important matters. First, the issues that are being neglected must be perceived as more important than concerns prompted by the allegations. Second, the accused must be perceived as neglecting these issues because of the charges. Third, the audience must perceive the accused as capable of positively addressing the neglected issues.

We believe that Clinton's use of transcendence met each of these criteria. First, polling data consistently showed that the public thought accusations against Clinton were either a private matter or inconsequential to his performance of duties. This attitude remained so even when the public believed he had broken the law! As such, one could argue that the allegations were considered less important than the issues facing the nation. Second, some (though not all) of the *New York Times* commentaries regularly complained that Clinton was negatively distracted from addressing issues like education and foreign policy due to allegations. Third, while we found no polling data indicating the public's confidence in Clinton's ability to address particular issues, we would still argue that the public believed he was capable of such leadership. The strength of his job approval ratings allows such an inference. His performance as president was certainly perceived in a positive way. One could argue that a positive perception of performance would be accompanied by a positive perception of ability.

As such, this analysis confirms Benoit and Wells' (1998) three criteria for transcendence rooted in the argument that accusations are distractions from more important matters. We would add one more extension to our understanding of transcendence. For a rhetor to successfully claim that the subject of accusations is "private," or nobody else's business, the public should agree that the matter is private.

Clinton successfully met the privacy criteria in both the Flowers and Lewinsky scandals. Of course, claiming marital privacy was not his only strategy used in these cases, but in both matters the majority of the public agreed that his marital problems were between him and Hillary. However, if a politician were to embezzle public monies, he/she might not be able to claim that his/her subsequent purchases were a private matter. The public may well consider actions taken using public money as a public concern. In such a case, a claim of privacy would probably be ineffective.

This study also adds to our understanding of mortification and corrective action. Benoit and Brinson (1994) found that AT&T tried to shift blame for an extensive east coast service interruption to lower-level employees. This strategy was flatly rejected by the public, which was outraged at the attempt. Ultimately, AT&T executives decided to run full-page advertisements in prominent east coast papers expressing mortification and promising corrective action. Indeed, the headline of the ad proclaimed "Apologies are Not Enough." This decision was well received.

Likewise, Clinton used the mortification/corrective action couplet effectively in the wake of his admission of an inappropriate relationship with Monica Lewinsky. We submit that mortification should usually be tied to corrective action. This is because of the expectations of the audience. An audience that is offended sufficiently to require an apology would probably also require some explanation of how the misdeed will be avoided in the future. We do realize that the two represent wholly different types of statements, one expressing regret, the other proposing ways to avoid repetition. However, when a misdeed is admitted, the rhetor should be morally obligated to outline ways to avoid performing the misdeed again. In this sense, the mortification could function to improve the situations, rather than to simply "purify" in the Burkean sense, making this type of communication truly useful.

This work demonstrated an augmentation of the attack accuser strategy that could be described as "victimization." In his Whitewater discourse, Clinton assailed his accusers: "I have been the subject, sir, of false charges. People saying things about me that are not true don't make my credibility an issue. They make their credibility an issue, not mine" (Clinton, 1994d). Likewise, on the *Today* show, Hillary Clinton said: "Bill and I have been accused of everything, including murder, by some of the very people who are behind these accusations" (H. Clinton, 1998). Both of these instances demonstrate how one can claim to have been victimized by the accusers. It is not hard to imagine that if an audience can be convinced that the accused has been treated unfairly, then the audience may sympathize with the accused and hold contempt for the accuser. Thus, attacking one's accuser is possible through victimization. Note that this use of "victimization" is quite different from Burke's similarly labeled "victimage," which is defined as shifting blame.

Finally, the study illuminated an expansion as well as some boundaries on the use of denial in image restoration discourse. When a rhetor is accused of wrongdoing, denial-plus-evidence is a possibility. For instance, when accused of mishandling the Whitewater matter, Clinton replied:

I certainly don't think I made a mistake in the initial investment. It was a perfectly honorable thing to do, and it was a perfectly legal thing to do. And I didn't make any money, I lost money. I paid my debts. And then later on, as you know, Hillary and I tried to make sure that the corporation was closed down in an appropriate way. (Clinton, 1994b)

Here, Clinton not only denied wrongdoing, but he also offered evidence for his denial. Thus, a rhetor can engage in denial and denial-plus-evidence.

Some boundaries for denial were discovered as well. One should deny wrongdoing *only* if one is absolutely sure that no proof of the misdeed exists. Perhaps this sounds a bit elementary, but it is sound advice for those who would deny having done something that, in fact, they did commit (e.g., Clinton's denials about Lewinsky, Reagan's denials of trading arms for hostages, Nixon's denials of knowledge of the Watergate break-in). Undoudtedly, one would surmise, these three rhetors proceeded as though no proof of wrongdoing would materialize. They were wrong. Moreover, their images were damaged by revelations that they had lied. Of course, morally speaking, one should really only deny wrongdoing if one performed no misdeeds. We recognize that some believe dissembling is sometimes a necessary, legitimate form of persuasive defense (Bok, 1978). However, even these people should be advised not to deny that which is demonstrably true. Such lies, when discovered, will destroy their credibility.

Also, the studies demonstrated that denial could be employed for what we would call "secondary refutations" in image restoration discourse. For instance, as discussed in Chapter five, Clinton admitted to smoking marijuana, yet he denied lying to reporters about his drug use in previous interviews. In short, a rhetor may choose to admit a primary accusation while denying some secondary charge.

The study has provided new information about the effective use of some of Benoit's (1995a) image restoration strategies. It has offered an expanded understanding of transcendence, mortification and corrective action, attack accuser, and denial.

Utilization of Surrogates

Benoit and Wells (1998) found that surrogate, or "third party," persuasive defense could be an effective option for political figures under attack. In that study, they examined a *New York Times* advertisement that advanced arguments supporting the Clintons in the wake of the Whitewater allegations. Though the authors of the ad were probably partisan allies, Benoit and Wells found that Bill and Hillary probably benefited nonetheless because the ad would appear more objective than their own self-defense. They also found that Bill and Hillary helped each other rhetorically. Hillary placed responsibility for their investments squarely on herself through her first-person descriptions of the deeds. Likewise, Bill bolstered Hillary. In this way, they performed surrogate image repair for each other.

Benoit and Wells' (1998) theoretical understanding of surrogates has some applicability to this study. Indeed, when others speak on behalf of an accused person, their rhetoric is by definition less self-interested, albeit not objective. They are attempting to repair the image of the accused, not themselves. However, the discourse of Hillary Rodham Clinton, Tom Lantos, Jack Quinn, and Mack McLarty reveal a boundary on surrogate effectiveness. In the advertisement examined by Benoit and Wells, the rhetors represented themselves as concerned citizens, and thus, may have been perceived as more objective and disinterested than Clinton's defenders in those instances. In contrast, Hillary, Lantos, Quinn, and McLarty were inextricably tied to the president personally and professionally. Hillary was Clinton's wife; Lantos, a senior Democratic member of Congress; Quinn the White House Counsel; and McLarty, the White House Chief of Staff and a Clinton friend since childhood. The public would probably view these rhetors as much less objective than an ad hoc committee assembled from the outside to provide persuasive defense. Of course, they were, by definition, more objective and less self-interested than the president. Each of these people could be highly interested in Clinton's positive image, but not as interested as Clinton himself.

Notably, each of these rhetors failed in their image repair duties. As such, one may conclude that a surrogate is more effective when the public perceives that the surrogate is at least reasonably independent (personally, politically, and professionally) of the accused.

It is also interesting to note the role of attacks among surrogates. Clinton used attack accuser as a major strategy only once: in his August 17, 1998, address to the nation wherein he admitted to his relationship with Monica Lewinsky. In all other situations, including his other remarks concerning Lewinsky, he either avoided attacking altogether or used it only as a minor strategy.

In sharp contrast, Hillary Rodham Clinton, Jack Quinn, and Tom Lantos each relied on attack accuser as a major strategy. This is not to say that attacking the accuser is an ineffective strategy, especially given the damaging evidence these particular surrogates faced. We have seen in this work that it can be most effective. However, this reliance on attacking supports the notion that a surrogate may be more likely to attack accusers than the accused person. Of course, Mack McLarty did not attack accusers. However, this can be attributed to that rhetorical situation, which was explicitly apologetic. These findings are consistent with Trent and Friedenberg's (1995) claim that political campaign surrogates can make statements that the candidates might like to say themselves, but are prevented by political expedience. They provided examples: George Bush surrogate Mary Matalin attacked Bill Clinton for being a "philandering, pot-smoking, draft dodger"; Bill Clinton surrogate Maxine Waters called George Bush a "racist" (p. 172). This study adds to this particular understanding of surrogates by expanding the application to non-campaign discourse.

Another difference found between Clinton and his surrogates involves transcendence. Clinton used this strategy, usually to a major extent, in each of the scandals (except for the marijuana discourse which was very limited in length). In contrast, of the surrogates, only Quinn and Lantos used transcendence, and in that instance only to a minor extent. However, it could be that transcendence was not an appropriate strategy for Hillary and McLarty. Had Hillary used transcendence, she may have appeared equivocal in her denial of Bill's infidelity. She was probably serving the unique surrogate role of a wife who believed her husband (the relative importance of the allegations notwithstanding). As such, transcendence would not have been appropriate. McLarty probably avoided transcendence because of the apologetic nature of the speech. To argue that the misdeeds in question were not that important might have detracted from the mortification he wanted to express. Arguably, there is no logical reason why these two surrogates could not have used transcendence more. However, if their primary missions were to deny wrongdoing (Hillary) or express mortification (McLarty), then less reliance on transcendence was proper.

Conversely, the politician, in this case Clinton, can safely make transcendence claims because (a) such discourse tends not to violate any politically expedient criteria (like an aggressive attack), and (b) such discourse may even be expected of a politician of high stature. The business of such politicians could surely be described as more important than scandalous accusations. These reasons explain why the accused should engage in transcendence more than a surrogate. Again, however, there is no theoretical reason why a surrogate should not employ transcendence.

Finally, one notable similarity between surrogates and accusees exists. Both can deny wrongdoing. This may not be surprising because the avoidance of damage to the accused's reputation is a shared goal. Given this, we cannot imagine a rhetorical reason why one would be more likely to deny than the other. The surrogate and the accused share the goal of disassociating wrongdoing from the politician. Clinton, Hillary Rodham Clinton, Jack Quinn, Tom Lantos, and Mack McLarty (even though his discourse was largely mortifying) each did this.

The implications concerning surrogates are four-fold. First, surrogates who are perceived as personally, politically, and professionally independent of the accused are probably more effective than those closely tied to the accused. Second, by nature, surrogates are better able to attack accusers. Third, by nature, the accused is more likely to engage in transcendence than the surrogate, especially if the accused performs important duties. Finally, the accused are just as likely as their surrogates to engage in denial of wrongdoing.

Style

Another implication of this study is the rhetorical style Clinton adopted. Clinton tended to begin his persuasive defenses with denials. This tendency is shared by other previously studied political rhetors, Presidents Nixon and Reagan and Speaker Newt Gingrich. Since politicians rely on the good will of the electorate, it could be that denial of wrongdoing is a politician's immediate, reflexive response. Each of these communicators demonstrated a reluctance to admit wrongdoing until incontrovertible evidence was produced. Of course, their uniform use of denial is not the only rhetorical feature worth noting. A comparison of Clinton with these other notable rhetors is in order. See Table 9.2.

Clinton and Nixon both made widespread use of transcendence. Clinton primarily declared that the allegations against him paled in importance next to the issues facing the country. This type of transcendence Benoit (1982) called refocusing attention to policy issues. When Nixon stressed confidentiality and executive privilege he transcended again, claiming that conversations between his staff and himself were sacrosanct because they allowed

Table 9.2
Breakdown of Nixon, Reagan, and Gingrich Strategies

Scandal	Accusation	Major Strategy	Minor Strategy
Nixon*	break-in/cover-up	BL, CN, EI, CO	RE, JD
			EP, MD, SB
			QT
Reagan	negotiate with terrorists	SD, GI, BL	AA, DI, MO, CA
Gingrich	greedy	GI, BL	-
	conflict of interests	SD	-
		AA, CA	-

Abbreviation Key: SD-simple denial, SB-shift blame, DI-differentiation, AA-attack accuser, CA-corrective action, MO-mortification, BL-bolstering, GI-good intentions

*Study of Nixon was conducted before Benoit's (1995a) theory of image restoration strategies was advanced. The abbreviations that follow are converted to be compatible with these strategies:

TR/CN-emphasizing confidentiality=transcendence, EI-emphasizing investigations=bolstering, CO-emphasizing cooperation=bolstering, RE-refocusing attention=transcendence, JD-indicting John Dean=attack accuser, EP-emphasizing executive privilege=transcendence, QT-quoting tapes=minimize

for the proper execution of the people's affairs. Moreover, Clinton argued that he needed to do what he was elected to do while Nixon emphasized his election mandate to complete his work in office. These are both examples of transcendence as well. Clinton and Nixon both relied on this strategy.

Nixon and Clinton pointed to their cooperation with investigators as a way to bolster their images. Both also attacked their accusers.

Of course, Nixon's discourse could not rescue his presidency, while Clinton's discourse has been effective. One possible explanation is that Nixon's troubles (e.g., the break-in and the tapes) were more damning than the various allegations that faced Clinton. Additionally, the public believed Clinton's transgressions were a private, sexual matter (the legal aspects notwithstanding). Perhaps if Nixon had expressed mortification and corrective action following the Watergate break-in he could have withstood the crisis. As it turned out, the incident became more ominous with every attempt to deny and cover up the deed. Another possible explanation could be that in 1998 the United States was at peace and in excellent economic shape, whereas in 1974 the country was at the end of a highly unpopular war and in an economic recession. While we cannot be certain of the reason, we do know that Nixon ultimately failed to repair his image.

Like Clinton, Reagan denied wrongdoing until evidence required that he admit his violations. Moreover, they both engaged in mortification, and subsequently, corrective action. This couplet was effective for both rhetors. The two also shared the use of the good intentions strategy. When faced with proof of wrongdoing, they both claimed to have performed the deeds in order to achieve something positive. Clinton said he lied about his relationship with Monica Lewinsky in order to protect his family. Reagan allowed the sale of arms to Iran in order to bring home American hostages. Both Clinton and Reagan bolstered themselves to repair their images. Notably, Reagan used no transcendence while Clinton used it liberally. In the end, mortification and corrective action were wise choices as they both retained high approval ratings.

Benoit, Gullifor, and Panici (1991) noted that Reagan's repair would have been even stronger had he confessed the misdeed early in the crisis. We are prepared to say the same of Clinton. However, one cannot deny the rhetorical success the two achieved. This comparison allows an important distinction between personal and official wrongdoing. Clinton admitted personal wrongdoing and subsequently suffered damage to his personal image while maintaining a high job approval rating. On the other hand, Reagan admitted to official wrongdoing and managed to repair both his job approval rating and personal image, as Gallup (1987) indicated following Reagan's August 12, 1987, speech. This is a possible indicator that Americans are more willing to forgive (at a personal, nonofficial level) mistakes people make as officeholders than mistakes made in their personal lives. After all, Clinton's official approval was sustained while his personal level plummeted.

Clinton and Gingrich (book deal) shared some of the same strategies as well, including the propensity to deny. Of course, we have already commented that one should not deny that which is true. Furthermore, if misdeeds had been performed, the rhetor would be wise to admit the mistake and promise corrective action. Clinton conformed to this concept. In contrast, Gingrich made the choice to promise corrective action without admitting wrongdoing. This was not sound. When one promises to prevent recurrences of an unfortunate action, one implicitly admits to wrongdoing. As such, Gingrich was probably perceived as guilty, yet lacking contrition. Bill Clinton eventually chose to admit his mistakes and promise corrective action. In the end, Clinton's image repair was more successful than Gingrich's. One could argue that Clinton and Gingrich both succeeded by one important criteria: they both succeeded in retaining power despite their declines in personal favorability. However, for Gingrich that would be a dubious achievement given that his fate was tied to partisan allies. Moreover, all through Gingrich's tenure as Speaker, his image never recovered and he eventually lost power as well.

These comparisons between Clinton, Nixon, Reagan, and Gingrich show that denial is, at first, an attractive strategy for those accused of wrongdoing. Moreover, the strategies chosen by the four leaders had differences as well as similarities. Nixon and Gingrich made poor rhetorical choices. Reagan and Clinton, though they made poor choices early in their crises, eventually communicated more effectively.

Severity of Accusations

Another major implication of this study lies in the characteristics of the charges. The severity of charges leveled against a rhetor is just as important as the truth or falsity of the allegations. This is demonstrated rather blatantly by the marijuana issue. There may have been a time when admission of pot-smoking would have immediately disqualified a candidate as unfit to be president. However, by the 1992 election cycle, pot-smoking may have diminished as an issue. Recall that Clinton's admission failed to draw any substantial criticism in the *New York Times* commentary sections. This supports the notion that the public no longer considered marijuana use as unforgivable.

Of course, Clinton's admission on the matter stressed his minimal use of the drug, characterizing it as experimentation. Moreover, Clinton pointed out that then-Senator Albert Gore and Governor Bruce Babbitt had both admitted marijuana use to no outcry. It is possible that if Clinton had admitted to smoking pot on repeated occasions, over a long period of time, well into adulthood, then perhaps the public would have been more concerned. Supreme Court nominee Douglas Ginsburg's nomination was withdrawn due to his relatively recent drug use.

Clinton's youthful indiscretion of marijuana experimentation brought little wrath. This is particularly notable considering that his explanation of the matter (i.e., but I didn't inhale") was laughable, and became a household joke. Clearly, this demonstrates the importance of the severity of accusations in image repair.

The FBI files incident provides another example. While it was certainly wrong for the files to be obtained in the first place, there was no evidence that the files were actually used in a clandestine fashion. Had the files been used in such a corrupt manner, the allegations against Clinton would have been much more severe, perhaps justifying impeachment. Recall that Quinn and Lantos did not provide an effective defense for Clinton. Again, the lack of severity offset an ineffective image repair effort. The allegations did not lead to serious legal or political problems. These examples demon-strate that accusations without a high degree of gravity can be repaired more easily than those of a more serious nature.

Triangulation

We believe one of the strengths of this study lies in the evaluation crite-ria. Not only was the discourse subjected to examination for its inherent strengths, but also evaluated by two external criteria. The polling data indi-cated how well the strategies had been received in general. Then, the news-paper commentary clarified the meaning lurking behind the numbers. This triangulation allowed a deeper understanding of the effectiveness of the texts. However, one should note that pundits were generally out of touch with public opinion concerning Clinton's August 17, 1998, speech address-ing the Lewinsky matter.

Method Appropriateness

The studies contained herein have revealed that Benoit's (1995a) theory of image restoration strategies provides an appropriate means for studying defensive discourse in numerous and diverse contexts. The speech pro-vided by Clinton and his surrogates addressed allegations ranging from the highly personal (e.g., adultery, drug use) to the largely mundane (e.g., Whitewater). The method used here was helpful in describing Clinton's strategies in each of the applications.

Multiple Goals

Finally, one of the major discoveries of this project was the realization that the image repair strategies could be used to maintain one's position, even when repairing one's image is not possible. This may be of particular importance in the study of political communication. The Monica Lewinsky scandal is illustrative. Clinton sought to (1) repair his image, (2) avoid polit-ical removal, and (3) escape legal conviction. Clearly, the rhetor may have multiple goals, and achieving all three may not be simultaneously possible. In these cases, *apologia* priorities must be set. For instance, Clinton chose to use a legalistic approach, stating things that he thought could be legally defensible, if not entirely forthcoming. The result was Clinton's assertion that his testimony was "legally accurate," rather than an all-out apology for deceit. He stuck to his legal guns, and escaped conviction by the United

States Senate. However, as the polls showed, the public respected him less as a person following those remarks.

As the public threshold for tolerating misfeasance increases, the politician's rhetorical goal may evolve from maintenance of a positive reputation to avoidance of official rejection by the voters and legal consequences.

Conclusion

Briefly, this study raised seven major implications. First, it expanded our understanding of the effectiveness of various image repair strategies. Second, it shed light on our understanding of surrogates in image repair. Third, it denoted Clinton's stylistic characteristics and compared these with those of Presidents Nixon and Reagan and Speaker Gingrich. Fourth, it demonstrated clearly that the severity of the charges a rhetor faces is just as important as the strategies chosen to address those charges. Fifth, evaluations of rhetorical strategies can be augmented by two criteria: polling data, which provides the means for generalizations about reactions; and newspaper commentary, which provides insight into the polling data. This triangulation allows a richer understanding of audience response. Sixth, Benoit's method is appropriate for studying image repair in large and diverse discourse sets. Finally, the image restoration strategies studied in these texts can be used to maintain power (read: avoid punishment) even when one's image is beyond repair.

LIMITATIONS

While each of these studies has been conducted in a systematic, consistent fashion, some limitations do apply. First, the texts examined herein do not represent everything that Clinton had to say about these matters. However, they were the most notable and/or extensive remarks he made about each of the accusations. Likewise, the polling data and newspaper commentaries had limitations in themselves. Polling firms like Gallup and Roper use probability samples and generally conduct reputable research. However, the results of the one or two polls attendant to some of my effectiveness questions need to be understood as a limited set of data. In the same fashion, the *New York Times* is not the only newspaper that printed reactions to the various scandals. Newspapers from all across the nation, in various types of metropolitan and rural areas might have radically different commentary.

Second, we would argue that Clinton's discourse was surely the most important source of influence on the public in these matters. Moreover, the key to his rhetorical success lies in transcendence. However, one might question how effective his transcendence would have been during an economic recession (as opposed to the prosperity over which he presides). In short, would his discourse have been just as effective had the country not been so content? This study could not answer that question.

FUTURE RESEARCH

The limitations discussed above are a good starting point for suggesting future research. Scholars may want to study Clinton's remarks made in less noteworthy contexts such as impromptu remarks made at White House photo opportunities and press conferences dedicated to unrelated matters. Also, the lack of research about surrogates' roles in repairing a person's (politician or otherwise) image merits much more exploration.

Moreover, research should examine what effect a poor economy or other policy crisis has on the rhetor's ability to use transcendence effectively. Moreover, the rhetorical limits of transcendence would be a fruitful area for inquiry in general.

Future research could also broaden the subjects studied. Presidents, quite justifiably, have been the topic of much image repair discourse. However, other political figures merit research as well. Studies have addressed Senator Ted Kennedy (Ling, 1970) and House Speaker Newt Gingrich (Kennedy & Benoit, 1997). Other political notables worthy of study include: Vice President Albert Gore's response to charges that he violated campaign finance laws; Texas Senator Phil Gramm's answers to charges that he invested in a morally licentious film; House Judiciary Committee Chairman Henry Hyde's remarks following revelations of past adultery; and Tennessee State Senate candidate "Low Tax" Looper's response to allegations that he killed his opponent.

Of course, the list of politicians to be studied has tremendous potential at all levels of government: federal, state, county, and municipal. Scholars should dedicate themselves to understanding image restoration in these many diverse contexts.

FINAL THOUGHT

The overall conclusion of this project is that President Bill Clinton is a very gifted communicator. In the face of serious accusations, he has repeatedly been able to defend himself and maintain popular support. This view is incontrovertible.

However, we want the reader to understand something plainly. Though he is an effective rhetor, we have found his means of defense highly immoral ever since he entered the national spotlight as a candidate for the Democratic nomination for the presidency. He has shown repeatedly that he is willing to: (1) omit material facts, (2) bend the meaning of specific terms incredibly, (3) engage in petty evasiveness, and (4) lie explicitly. He is the "poster boy" for the twisted, dishonest use of language.

To the trite counter of some who would say, "We elected him president, not pope," we would argue that we elected a used car salesman (our apologies to previously driven automobile entrepreneurs). Surely, past presidents have committed their own sins: racism, financial corruption, marital infidelity, lying. However, none of them used their means of communication so unashamedly to reduce the presidency to such a shameful stature. Even Richard Nixon had the decency to resign rather than lose all dignity.

To our children and future grandchildren and great-grandchildren who find this dusty volume among the family heirlooms, we state our position. What is persuasive is not always right.

Bibliography

A crisis from petty sources. (1998, January 22). *New York Times,* p. A28.

Abadi, A. (1990). The speech act of apology in political life. *Journal of Pragmatics, 14,* 467–471.

Ackerman, B. (1998, September 14). What Ken Starr neglected to tell us. *New York Times,* p. A31.

Aurichio, A. (1998, August 22). Was Clinton's confession too little or too much? *New York Times*, p. A14.

Baker, B. & Bard, M. (1998, January 29). Clinton's TV ratings. http://com.bu.edu/comnews/012998.html.

Baker, R. (1992, January 28). Before much longer, *New York Times,* p. A21.

Baker, R. (1996, June 25). Itching for a file. *New York Times,* p. A21.

Baker, R. (1998, January 23). Is this the end of Rico? *New York Times,* p. A21.

Baker, T. (1998, August 21). Blameless Republicans? *New York Times,* p. A24.

Balz, D. & Broder, D. S. (1992, February 14). Democrats talk of new candidates. *Washington Post,* p. A1.

Becker, E. (1992, February 14). Vietnam again haunts politics. *New York Times,* p. A29.

Benoit, W. L. (1982). Richard M. Nixon's rhetorical strategies in his public statements on Watergate. *Southern Speech Communication Journal, 47,* 192–211.

Benoit, W. L. (1988). Senator Edward M. Kennedy and the Chappaquidick tragedy. In H. R. Ryan (Ed.), *Oratorical encounters: Selected studies and sources of twentieth-century political accusations and apologies* (pp. 187–200). Westport, CT: Greenwood.

Benoit, W. L. (1995a). *Accounts, excuses, and apologies: A theory of image restoration strategies.* Albany: State University of New York Press.

Benoit, W. L. (1995b). Sears' repair of its auto service image: Image restoration discourse in the corporate sector. *Communication Studies, 46,* 89–105.

Benoit, W. L. (1997). Hugh Grant's image restoration discourse: An actor apologizes. *Communication Quarterly, 45,* 251–267.

Benoit, W. L. & Anderson, K. K. (1996). Blending politics and entertainment: Dan Quayle versus Murphy Brown. *Southern Communication Journal, 62,* 73–85.

Benoit, W. L. & Brinson, S. L. (1994). AT&T: "Apologies are not enough." *Communication Quarterly, 42,* 75–88.

Benoit, W. L. & Czerwinski, A. (1997). A critical analysis of USAir's image repair discourse. *Business Communication Quarterly, 60,* 38–57.

Benoit, W. L. & Drew, S. (1997). Appropriateness and effectiveness of image repair strategies. *Communication Reports, 10,* 153–163.

Benoit, W. L., Gullifor, P., & Panici, D. A. (1991). President Reagan's defensive discourse on the Iran-Contra affair. *Communication Studies, 42,* 272–294.

Benoit, W. L. & Hanczor, R. S. (1994). The Tonya Harding controversy: An analysis of image restoration strategies. *Communication Quarterly, 42,* 416–433.

Benoit, W. L. & Nill, D. M. (1998). Oliver Stone's defense of *JFK. Communication Quarterly, 46,* 127–143.

Benoit, W. L. & Wells, W. T. (1998). An analysis of three image restoration discourses on Whitewater. *Journal of Public Advocacy, 3,* 21–37.

Betrayal and embarrassment. (1998, August 19). *New York Times,* p. A30.

Bill Clinton meets his enemy. (1998, August 11). *New York Times,* p. A23.

Bill Clinton's Vietnam test. (1992, February 14). *New York Times,* p. A28.

Birnbaum, J. H. (1992, February 6). Clinton received a Vietnam draft deferment for an ROTC program that he never joined. *Wall Street Journal,* p. A16.

Blair, C. (1984). From "All the President's Men" to every man for himself: The strategies of post-Watergate *apologia. Central States Speech Journal, 35,* 250–260.

Blaney, J. R. & Benoit, W. L. (1997). The persuasive defense of Jesus in the Gospel according to John. *Journal of Communication and Religion, 20,* 25–30.

Bok, S. (1978). *Lying: Moral choice and public life.* New York: Pantheon.

Bostdorff, D. M. (1996). Clinton's characteristic issue management style: Caution, conciliation, and conflict avoidance in the case of gays in the military. In R. E. Denton & R. L. Holloway (Eds.), *The Clinton presidency: Images, issues, and communication strategies* (pp. 189–224). Westport, CT: Praeger.

Brenders, D. A., & Fabj, V. A. (1993). Perceived control and the Clinton presidency. *American Behavioral Scientist, 37,* 211–224.

Brinson, S. L. & Benoit, W. L. (1996). Dow Corning's image repair strategies in the breast implant crisis. *Communication Quarterly, 44,* 29–41.

Brock, D. (1994, June). The Travelgate cover-up. *The American Spectator,* pp. 30–43.

Broder, D. S. & Edsall, T. B. (1992, February 13). Clinton releases '69 letter on his draft deferment. *Washington Post,* p. A1.

Brummett, B. (1975). Presidential substance: The address of August 15, 1973. *Western Speech Communication, 39,* 249–259.

Burke, K. (1969). *A rhetoric of motives.* Berkeley: University of California Press.

Carlin, D. B. & Howard, C. C. (1994). Bill Clinton's campaigns for Governor of Arkansas: Prelude to a presidency. In S. A. Smith (Ed.), *Bill Clinton on stump, state, and stage: The rhetorical road to the White House* (pp. 13–22). Fayetteville: University of Arkansas Press.

Clark, R. A. & Delia, R. J. (1979). *Topoi* and rhetorical competence. *Quarterly Journal of Speech, 65,* 187–206.

Clinton, H. R. (1998, January 27). *The Today Show* [television program]. National Broadcasting Company.

Clinton, W. J. (1994a, January 3). Remarks by the president at the health care meeting. www.whitehouse.gov.

Clinton, W. J. (1994b, March 24). Press conference of the president. www.whitehouse.gov.

Clinton, W. J. (1994c, March 25). Remarks by the president upon departure. www.whitehouse.gov.

Clinton, W. J. (1994d, April 5). Remarks by the president in "Evening with the President." www.whitehouse.gov.

Clinton, W. J. (1994e, July 23). Remarks by the president to the pool. www.whitehouse.gov.

Clinton, W. J. (1998a, January 21). Excerpts of telephone interview of the president by *Roll Call.* www.whitehouse.gov.

Clinton, W. J. (1998b, January 21). Interview of the president by Jim Lehrer of *News Hour.* www.whitehouse.gov.

Clinton, W. J. (1998c, January 26). Remarks by the president at the After-School program event. www.whitehouse.gov.

Clinton, W. J. (1998d, August 17). Transcript of President Bill Clinton's televised address. www.cnn.com/allpolitics.

Clinton, W. J. (1998e, September 11). Transcript of President Clinton's Address to the White House Prayer Breakfast. www.conservativenews.org.

Clinton admits to smoking marijuana. (1992, March 29). Cable News Network.

Collins, C. A. & Clark, J. E. (1992). Jim Wright's resignation speech: De-legitimization or redemption? *Southern Communication Journal, 58,* 67–75.

Denton, R. E. & Holloway, R. L. (1996). Clinton and the town hall meetings: Mediated conversation and the risk of being "in touch." In R. E. Denton & R. L. Holloway (Eds.), *The Clinton presidency: Images, issues, and communication strategies* (pp. 17–42). Westport, CT: Praeger.

Devroy, A. (1993, October 7). Costs of Clinton travel firings still growing. *Washington Post,* p. A21.

Dowd, M. (1996, June 23). Chaos becomes you. *New York Times,* p. E13.

Dowd, M. (1998a, January 25). Not suitable for children. *New York Times,* p. 15.

Dowd, M. (1998b, January 28). The slander strategy. *New York Times,* p. A25.

Dowd, M. (1998c, August 19). Saturday night Bill. *New York Times,* p. A29.

Edsall, T. B. (1992a, February 11). In south, hope—and unease—over Clinton. *Washington Post,* p. A8.

Edsall, T. B. (1992b, March 30). Clinton admits '60s marijuana use. *Washington Post,* p. A1.

Eisenberg, D. (1992, January 28). Letter to the editor. *New York Times,* p. A20.

Eisner, S. (1998, September 15). Frailties, not crimes. *New York Times,* p. A26.

For George Bush and Bill Clinton. (1992, April 5). *New York Times,* p. 16.

Forbes, S. (1996, July 15). Should be an impeachable offense. *Forbes,* p. 23.

Foster, R. B. (1998, September 15). A higher standard. *New York Times,* p. A26.

Friedman, T. L. (1998, January 27). Character suicide. *New York Times,* p. A19.

Froomkin, D. (1998a, May 12). Untangling Whitewater. www.washingtonpost.com/wp-srv/politics/special/whitewater/whitewater.htm.

Froomkin, D. (1998b, August 26). Frequently asked questions. www.washingtonpost.com/wp-srv/politics/special/clinton/faq.htm.

Gallup Report (1987, September). No. 264, pp. 16–25.

Gallup Organization (1992, February 4–6). Poll of Democratic voter preference.

Gelb, L. (1992, January 17). Journalistic cannibals. *New York Times,* p. A21.

Gergen, D. (1998, March 30). Defining democracy down: Bill Clinton's glowing poll numbers tell only one piece of the story. *U.S. News & World Report, 124,* p. 86.

Get the candidates. (1992, March 31). *New York Times,* p. A20.

Getz, G. C. (1994). Rhetoric and ritual in the Arkansas inaugural addresses. In S. A. Smith (Ed.), *Bill Clinton on stump, state, and stage: The rhetorical road to the White House* (pp. 23–51). Fayetteville: University of Arkansas Press.

Gold, E. R. (1978). Political *apologia:* The ritual of self-defense. *Communication Monographs, 45,* 306–316.

Hacker, K. L. (1996). Virtual democracy: A critique of the Clinton Administration citizen–White House electronic mail system. In Denton, R. E., & Holloway, R. L. (eds). (1996). *The Clinton presidency: Images, issues, and communication strategies.* Westport, CT: Praeger.

Hardy, R., Ph.D. (1998, November 1). Personal communication.

Harrell, J., Ware, B. L. & Linkugel, W. A. (1975). Failure of apology in American politics: Nixon on Watergate. *Speech Monographs, 42,* 245–261.

Hatch, O. (1996, June 19). *Larry King Live* [television program]. Cable News Network, Inc.

Hearit, K. M. (1995). "Mistakes were made": Organizations, *apologia,* and crises of social legitimacy. *Communication Studies, 46,* 1–17.

Herbeck, D. A. (1994). Presidential debate as political ritual: Clinton vs. Bush vs. Dole. In S. A. Smith (Ed.), *Bill Clinton on stump, state, and stage: The rhetorical road to the White House* (pp. 249–272). Fayetteville: University of Arkansas Press.

Herbert, B. (1998a, January 25). Suspension of belief. *New York Times,* p. 15.

Herbert, B. (1998b, January 29). The feminist dilemma. *New York Times,* p. A23.

Herbert, B. (1998c, August 20). Clinton on the wire. *New York Times,* p. A23.

Holloway, R. L. (1996). The Clintons and the health care crisis: Opportunity lost, promise unfulfilled. In R. E. Denton & R. L. Holloway (Eds.), *The Clinton presidency: Images, issues, and communication strategies* (pp. 159–188). Westport, CT: Praeger.

Hugick, L. (1992, February). Gallup/CNN/USA Today: New Hampshire polls. *Gallup Poll Monthly,* pp. 34–40.

Huxman, S. S. & Bruce, D. B. (1995). Toward a dynamic generic framework of *apologia:* A case study of Dow Chemical, Vietnam, and the napalm controversy. *Communication Studies, 46,* 57–72.

Janet Reno's shameful delay. (1994, January 7). *New York Times,* p. A30.

Justice or mercy for Bill Clinton? (1998, September 14). *New York Times,* p. A32.

Kahl, M. (1984). *Blind Ambition* culminates in *Lost Honor:* A comparative analysis of John Dean's apologetic strategies. *Central States Speech Journal, 35,* 239–250.

Katula, R. A. (1975). The apology of Richard M. Nixon. *Today's Speech, 23,* 1–6.

Katz, L. (1998, August 19). All deceptions are not equal. *New York Times,* p. A29.

Kennedy, K. A. & Benoit, W. L. (1997). The Newt Gingrich book deal controversy: Self-defense rhetoric. *Southern Communication Journal, 63,* 197–216.

Kirby, R. W. (1998, January 24). Starr inquiry has crossed the line of decency. *New York Times,* p. A14.

Klein, J. (1992, February 17). The Democrats in New Hampshire. *New York,* pp. 14–15.

Klinger, W. (1996, June 19). *Larry King Live* [television program]. Cable News Network, Inc.

Kurtz, H. (1992, February 14). Candidates zero in with final ad barrage. *Washington Post,* p. A18.

Lantos, T. (1996, June 19). *Larry King Live* [television program]. Cable News Network, Inc.

Leach, J. A. (1993, December 31). A special counsel for Whitewater. *Washington Post,* p. A21.

Lentz, T. M. (1994). The voice of concern and concern for the voice. In S. A. Smith (Ed.), *Bill Clinton on stump, state, and stage: The rhetorical road to the White House* (pp. 133–149). Fayetteville: University of Arkansas Press.

Lewis, A. (1994, August 5). The grassy knoll. *New York Times.* p. A25.

Lewis, A. (1998, January 26). Lord high executioner. *New York Times,* p. A19.

Ling, D. A. (1970). A pentadic analysis of Senator Edward Kennedy's address to the people of Massachussetts, July 25, 1969. *The Central States Speech Journal, 21,* 81–86.

Linkugel, W. A. & Razak, N. (1969). Sam Houston's speech of self-defense in the House of Representatives. *Southern Speech Journal, 34,* 263–275.

Listening to the President. (1998, January 27). *New York Times,* p. A18.

Llewellyn, J. T. (1994). Bill Clinton's stump speaking: Persuasion through identification. In S. A. Smith (Ed.), *Bill Clinton on stump, state, and stage: The rhetorical road to the White House* (pp. 52–72). Fayetteville: University of Arkansas Press.

Marlow, G. R. (1994). Dodging charges and charges of dodging: Bill Clinton's defense on the character issue. In S. A. Smith (Ed.), *Bill Clinton on stump, state, and stage: The rhetorical road to the White House* (pp. 150–162). Fayetteville: University of Arkansas Press.

McClain, P. (1998, August 19). Faustian bargain. *New York Times,* p. A28.

McDougall, W. A. (1992, February 17). What we do for our country. *New York Times,* p. A27.

McGrory, M. (1992, February 11). The front-runner stumbles. *Washington Post,* p. A2.

McGuckin, H. E. (1968). A value analysis of Richard Nixon's 1952 campaign-fund speech. *The Southern Speech Journal, 33,* 259–269.

McLarty, M. (1993, July 2). Press briefing by White House Chief of Staff Mack McLarty. www.whitehouse.gov.

McManus, T. K. (1998, September 15). White House workplace. *New York Times,* p. A26.

Mink, G. (1998, August 18). Should the truth faze feminists? *New York Times,* p. A23.

Morello, J. T. (1979). The public apology of a private matter: Representative Wayne Hays' address to Congress. *Speaker and Gavel, 16,* 19–26.

Muir, J. K. (1994). Clinton goes to town hall. In S. A. Smith (Ed.), *Bill Clinton on stump, state, and stage: The rhetorical road to the White House* (pp. 341–364). Fayetteville: University of Arkansas Press.

Murphy, J. M. (1997). Inventing authority: Bill Clinton, Martin Luther King, Jr., and the orchestration of rhetorical traditions. *Quarterly Journal of Speech, 83,* 71–89.

Newman, R. P. (1970). Under the veneer: Nixon's Vietnam speech of November 3, 1969. *Quarterly Journal of Speech, 56,* 168–178.

Nightline. (1992, February 12). T. Bettag, Executive Producer. Washington, DC: American Broadcasting Company.

Palmer, N. (1998, August 19). The world waits. *New York Times,* p. A30.

Pelofsky, L. H. (1998, January 29). What Mr. Starr wants. *New York Times,* p. A22.

Poll: More Americans satisfied with Clinton's explanation. (1998, August 17). www.cnn.com/allpolitics.

Polls show job approval not hurt by Clinton confession. (1998, August 18). www.cnn.com/allpolitics.

Procter, D. E. & Ritter, K. (1996). Inaugurating the Clinton presidency: Regenerative rhetoric and the American community. In R. E. Denton & R. L. Holloway (Eds.), *The Clinton presidency: Images, issues, and communication strategies* (pp. 1–16). Westport, CT: Praeger.

Public Opinion Online (1992, September 30). Marijuana poll conducted September 22–24, 1992.

Public Opinion Online (1994, March 31). Whitewater poll conducted March 25–27, 1994.

Public Opinion Online (1994b, August). Whitewater poll conducted August 5–7, 1994.

Public Opinion Online (1994c, August). Whitewater poll conducted August 8–9, 1994.

Public Opinion Online (1996a, January 16). Travel Office poll conducted January 10–11, 1996.

Public Opinion Online (1996b, June 29). FBI files poll conducted June 27–28, 1996.

Public Opinion Online (1996c, July 1). FBI files poll conducted June 27–30, 1996.

Public Opinion Online (1998a, February). Monica Lewinsky poll conducted February 1, 1998.

Public Opinion Online (1998b, September 25). Ken Starr poll conducted September 23–24, 1998.

Public wants Clinton censured, but not removed. (1998, September 13). www.cnn.com/allpolitics.

Quindlen, A. (1992a, February 16). Wounded in battle. *New York Times,* p. E15.

Quindlen, A. (1992b, April 1). Just say yes. *New York Times,* p. A25.

Quinn, J. (1996, June 19). *Larry King Live* [television program]. Cable News Network, Inc.

Rancorous diversions in Congress. (1998, September 18). *New York Times,* p. A28.

Rich, F. (1998a, January 24). All Monica all the time. *New York Times,* p. A15.

Rich, F. (1998b, January 28). Full court press. *New York Times,* p. A25.

Rich, F. (1998c, January 31). Hillary's double agents. *New York Times,* p. A15.

Rich, F. (1998d, August 19). Stain of the nation. *New York Times,* p. A29.

Richardson, E. (1998, September 18). Sometimes, evidence of guilt isn't enough. *New York Times,* p. A27.

Rivers, A. (1998, Aug. 19). Can the president, and country, now move on? *New York Times*, p. A30.

Roberts, S. (1992, February 3). Defusing the bombshell: Bill Clinton puts his antiscandal strategy into effect amid new charges about his private life. *U.S. News & World Report,* pp. 30–32.

Roiphe, K. (1998, September 15). Monica Lewinsky, career woman. *New York Times,* p. A31.

Rose, G. L. (1997). *The American presidency under siege.* Albany: State University of New York Press.

Rosenfield, L. W. (1968). A case study in speech criticism: The Nixon-Truman analog. *Speech Monographs, 35,* 435–450.

Rosenthal, A. M. (1992, April 3). New York and Clinton. *New York Times,* p. A29.

Rosenthal, A. M. (1998, September 18). The three questions. *New York Times,* p. A27.

Ryan, H. R. (1982). *Kategoria* and *apologia*: On their rhetorical criticism as a speech set. *Quarterly Journal of Speech, 68,* 256–261.

Safire, W. (1994a, January 6). Foster's ghost. *New York Times,* p. A21.

Safire, W. (1994b, August 4). The whole truth. *New York Times,* p. A23.

Safire, W. (1996, June 24). 3 scandals and out. *New York Times,* p. A15.

Safire, W. (1998a, January 26). Speechwriter's draft. *New York Times,* p. A19.

Safire, W. (1998b, January 29). Whose conspiracy? *New York Times,* p. A23.

Scammon, R. M. & McGillivray, A. V. (Eds.). (1993). *America Votes, 20* (pp. 49–53). Washington, DC: Congressional Quarterly.

Seib, P. (1994). Riding the roller coaster: Bill Clinton and the news media. In S. A. Smith (Ed.), *Bill Clinton on stump, state, and stage: The rhetorical road to the presidency* (pp. 273–291). Fayetteville: University of Arkansas Press.

Sellnow, T. L. & Ulmer, R. R. (1995). Ambiguous argument as advocacy in organizational crisis communication. *Argumentation and Advocacy, 31,* 138–150.

Shame at the White House. (1998, September 12). *New York Times,* p. A18.

Short, B. (1987). Comic book *apologia:* The "paranoid" rhetoric of Congressman George Hansen. *Western Journal of Speech Communication, 51,* 189–203.

60 Minutes (1992, January 26). CBS Television Network.

Smith, C. A. (1994). The Jeremiadic logic of Bill Clinton's policy speeches. In S. A. Smith (Ed.), *Bill Clinton on stump, state, and stage: The rhetorical road to the White House* (pp. 73–100). Fayetteville: University of Arkansas Press.

Smith, C. A. (1996). "Rough stretches and honest disagreements": Is Bill Clinton redefining the rhetorical presidency? In R. E. Denton & R. L. Holloway (Eds.), *The Clinton presidency: Images, issues, and communication strategies* (pp. 225–248). Westport, CT: Praeger.

Smith, J. M. (1998, January 26). When the truth hurts. *New York Times,* p. A19.

Smith, L. D. (1994). The New York convention: Bill Clinton and "A place called Hope." In S. A. Smith (Ed.), *Bill Clinton on stump, state, and stage: The rhetorical road to the White House* (pp. 201–222). Fayetteville: University of Arkansas Press.

State of the presidency. (1998, January 25). *New York Times,* p. 14.

Super Tuesday aftermath: Clinton surges ahead. (1992, March). *Gallup Poll Monthly,* pp. 18–20.

Taylor, S. (1998, February 2). The legal lowdown. *Newsweek,* pp. 48–49.

Tell the full story, Mr. President. (1998, January 23). *New York Times,* p. A20.

The candidates, on April 7. (1992, April 5). *New York Times,* p. 16.

The travel office report. (1993, July 4). *Washington Post,* p. C6.

Time for a special prosecutor. (1994, January 4). *New York Times,* p. A14.

Trent, J. S. & Friedenberg, R. V. (1992). *Political campaign communication: Principles and practices.* Westport, CT: Praeger.

Van Dyk, T. (1992, January 30). Clinton's middle class hang-up. *New York Times*, p. A21.

Vartabedian, R. A. (1985). From Checkers to Watergate: Richard Nixon and the art of contemporary *apologia. Speaker and Gavel, 22,* 52–61.

Ware, B. L. & Linkugel, W. A. (1973). They spoke in defense of themselves: On the generic criticism of *apologia. Quarterly Journal of Speech, 59,* 273–283.

Washington Post Online (1998, July 29). wp4.washingtonpost.com/wp-srv/national/longterm/wwtr/intro.

Will, G. F. (1992, April 2). . . . Or the buccaneers. *Washington Post,* p. A27.

Wilson, G. L. (1976). A strategy of explanation: Richard M. Nixon's August 8, 1974, resignation address. *Communication Quarterly, 24,* 14–20.

Wines, M. (1994, August 7). Boredom mixed with danger. *New York Times,* p. 26.

Wozniak, G. (1998, September 15). A Lewinsky apology. *New York Times,* p. A26.

Index

About the Authors

JOSEPH R. BLANEY is Assistant Professor of Communication at Illinois State University. He is the joint author, with W. L. Benoit and P. M. Pier, of *Campaign '96: A Functional Analysis of Acclaiming, Attacking, and Defending* (Praeger, 1998) and numerous articles on communication and rhetoric issues.

WILLIAM L. BENOIT is Professor of Communication at the University of Missouri. The author of six earlier books and almost 100 articles and book chapters, Professor Benoit's last book publication is *Seeing Spots* (Praeger, 1999).